Bird Songs of the Mesozoic

A L S O   B Y

DAVID BRENDAN HOPES

A Sense of the Morning

The Glacier's Daughters

Blood Rose

A Childhood in the Milky Way

Bird Songs
of the
Mesozoic

A Day Hiker's Guide to the Nearby Wild

. . . .

David Brendan Hopes

MILKWEED ⬤ EDITIONS

Published 2005 by Milkweed Editions
Printed in Canada
Cover and interior design by Christian Fünfhausen
Cover image, "Self-Portrait #5" (Polaroid/correction fluid), and interior images by Michael Carina.
The text of this book is set in Mrs. Eaves Regular.
05 06 07 08 09   5 4 3 2 1
First Edition

Milkweed Editions, a nonprofit publisher, gratefully acknowledges support from Emilie and Henry Buchwald; Bush Foundation; Cargill Value Investment; Timothy and Tara Clark Family Charitable Fund; DeL Corazón Family Fund; Dougherty Family Foundation; Ecolab Foundation; Joe B. Foster Family Foundation; General Mills Foundation; Jerome Foundation; Kathleen Jones; Constance B. Kunin; D. K. Light; Chris and Ann Malecek; McKnight Foundation; a grant from the Minnesota State Arts Board, through an appropriation by the Minnesota State Legislature, a grant from the National Endowment for the Arts, and private funders; Sheila C. Morgan; Laura Jane Musser Fund; an award from the National Endowment for the Arts, which believes that a great nation deserves great art; Navarre Corporation; Kate and Stuart Nielsen; Outagamie Charitable Foundation; Qwest Foundation; Debbie Reynolds; St. Paul Travelers Foundation; Ellen and Sheldon Sturgis; Surdna Foundation; Target Foundation; Gertrude Sexton Thompson Charitable Trust (George R. A. Johnson, Trustee); James R. Thorpe Foundation; Toro Foundation; Weyerhaeuser Family Foundation; and Xcel Energy Foundation.

Library of Congress Cataloging-in-Publication Data

Hopes, David B.
  Bird songs of the Mesozoic : a day hiker's guide to the nearby wild / David Brendan Hopes.
    p.   cm.
  ISBN-13: 978-1-571312-77-8 (pbk. : alk. paper)
  ISBN-10: 1-57131-277-3
  1. Nature. I. Title.
  QH81.H729 2005
  508—dc22   2004021870

This book is printed on acid-free paper.

MINNESOTA
STATE ARTS BOARD

NATIONAL
ENDOWMENT
FOR THE ARTS

To Dr. K. N. Blackmore

POET AND SCIENTIST

Bird Songs
of the Mesozoic

Bird Songs of the Mesozoic

Introduction

IT'S AUGUST, AND IN A FEW DAYS I will be standing in
front of a humanities class. I am a professor of literature
normally, and in a literature class, I do not have to stop
to explain distinctions between what is perceived by the
synthetic imagination and what by the analytic. In this
interdisciplinary class, interlarded with biology majors
and budding businesspersons, I do. I want to say to them,
"I will be telling you a story. Everything in the story is
true, even when it cannot be proven, even when it can be
'proved' to be wrong. And I do not mean that as a paradox, any more than it is a paradox that the moon should

3

be in the sky by day, or that we are fish and salamanders in our mothers' wombs before we are people." All the best and true stories begin, "Once upon a time." This is no less true of the book of nature than for a bedtime story, and everything we say is likely equally fantastic to whatever Power sits in the center of things and knows.

The important issue, in fact, is the quality of the story. I might even say "the quality of the telling." In my world a story that is told badly is untrue. I suspect it is the same for science—"the elegance of the proof" and all that—though a scientist might express it differently. Sometimes a person has to step out of a discipline to make it shimmer into perfect focus. In the humanities class mentioned above, one can talk all day about the effect of Darwinism on the nineteenth-century mind, with charts, graphs, citations, or one can read the "Dragons of the prime, / That tare each other in their slime" passage from Tennyson's "In Memoriam," which tells it in a moment. How many mediocre science students would become and stay engaged if their professor stopped midlecture, turned off the slides for a minute, and said, "Listen, I am trying to tell you a story"? How many whining poetasters would snap into song if their teacher handed back their poems and said, "Prove it"?

Long ago I sat in my grandmother's garden and listened while she recited poetry from her Irish heart or read it from a book that had the poets' portraits in vignettes on the top of the page. At the time I was a rabid and independent reader of schoolboy science books: *Wonders of the Universe, Boy's Book of Fossils,* and whatnot. I think I've recorded elsewhere that it never crossed my mind that her poems and my bits of science were different things. The poems were discoveries as a new species or an interesting pile of bones were discoveries, and in the poets' portraits I looked for the evidence of their having been afield, where the great mysteries were waiting to be confronted. Even as some people listen to Chopin and others to Merle Haggard, the world speaks in many voices so that everyone has a chance to hear.

The perceptive will have noticed that I am going the long way around to explain why a poet should be writing a nature book. The excuse is simple. Long ago, in my grandmother's garden, I learned two languages. When the world presents its wonders to me, I must pass them on, and when I do, I never know—initially, at least—which language I am speaking.

This book is about the portion of nature I see around me, the dragonflies that buzz into my studio, the opossum cornered in the garage, the cats asleep on the desk, impeding my progress even now as I write. The closest I've come in recent times to expeditions into the wilderness are day hikes off the Blue Ridge Parkway or hours of stealth on the herony banks of Beaver Lake, a ten-minute walk from my front door. Some day I will wander to Antarctica or the jungles of Brazil, though I expect what I will have to say then will not vary materially from what I have to say now, though maybe then I'll have more vivid examples.

Wilderness finds us where we are. A friend and I drove a

third friend to the airport in Greenville, South Carolina. On the way home we stopped at the Greenville Zoo. The blazing hot day was alive with children, and the children were loud, and what was interesting about their loudness was that, under the cages of the red pandas, in the shadows of condors, the children were pointing to merry creatures they saw every day of their lives and bellowing, "Look! Look! A squirrel!" I knew what they were thinking. They were thinking, "Wait, wild animals have lived in my backyard forever, and I never gave them credit!"

At my studio the other day, my studio mate, Jenny, the fabric artist, knocked on my door and said, "Do you want to see a big praying mantis? It's on my mug." I did. I went to her studio, and there was a lovely pale brown mantis perched on her coffee mug, swiveling her head in a quizzical, almost catlike way. I thought Jenny had meant what she said, that she wanted to share the sight of an extraordinary creature, but she began to ask if I didn't think the mantis would be happier outside, and I realized she wanted to get rid of it, but was afraid to come near it and didn't want to sound all girly about asking me to remove a big bug from her mug. I lifted the creature up—it had real heft to it—and dropped it out the window. Jenny asked if it could fly, and the mantis had fallen about ten inches when she proved that she could. I looked at Jenny as I left her space. She was shaken and exultant. I might as well have shooed a jaguar away from her.

The title of this collection of essays is borrowed from a band that used to play locally. I Googled the band in preparation for thanking them, and found they are still at it, still churning out fascinating CDs with the best cover art in the world. One night I heard them in a little Lexington Avenue café called Vincent's Ear. They were playing experimental music on a series of synthesizers. Sometimes it was irritating, as anything new might be, but more often the music was strange and wonderful, summoning to mind dinosaurian forests, unthinkable throats ringing with the calls of birds vanished not only from the world, but almost from the imagination, bell-like, metallic, honeyed and voluptuous. You could read the musicians' faces when they happened upon something particularly fine: lamentations of hunger, arias of lust, chants of possession and inquiry, strange staccato outbursts of delight. I hope that's what it really sounded like back then, among the cycads and the carnosaurs. Longing tells me it must have.

OK, now I am telling you a story—

On the Right-of-Way

THE DAY WAS A BLAST FURNACE, and evening approaches still steaming. I came to my studio to paint, but the first thing that must be done is to rush through the breathless brown space to the back door, fling it open so the second-floor factory loft can ventilate. I lean against the balcony railing while the breeze edges leisurely in at my back. Big yellow swallowtails glide close to the wall of the building, then black ones following like willful shadows, riding a current detectable only by them. Great spiders weave, or lie in wait, or catch my movement in their incomprehensible eyes.

Thirty feet below, a rabbit dines on grass and herbs shouldered up through the pavement. Since I am here to paint, I notice the rabbit would make a good composition— brown (a brown you would reproduce by mixing raw umber, titan buff, touches of iron oxide or oxide yellow till you got it right) amid dusty viridian and pale gray, the yellow suns of goatsbeard overhanging his soft body and the hard gray edges of the concrete. The pokeweed is seven feet tall. A thistle leans against a roof. The Queen Anne's lace is not far behind.

Over my head in the eaves is the scrabbling of a hive— do they call it a hive? A nest, anyway—of carpenter bees. I should tell the landladies about this someday. They can't be good for the roof. A few soldiers still patrol the heavy golden air, but they're settling down in the old wood where they will scrabble and scrape all night like a tiny dog in a box. Swallows fill the air above the old rendering plant, dipping down in the space between my building and the next, grazing the top of the rabbit's ears as if they were trying to play with it.

Two ducks flap from the French Broad River toward town. They are quacking at each other. I wonder if ducks always quack as they fly, or if this time I am just close enough to hear them. What they would want in town, why they would be abandoning the cool flowing greenness of the river, the safety of the overhanging trees, I can't imagine. Perhaps some child's handout of bread.

The flash on the wall is a blue-lined skink, electric blue, like a tiny lightning bolt hurled across the bricks in full sun. So long as I arrive in daylight, I can count on catching the skink watching me from the door frame with its shallow black eyes like the eyes of a shark. What is it looking at with such beady concentration? A lizard's critique of my paintings would be worth having.

THOUGH THE CANDLE-STORE ladies are organizing their Saturday candle sale downstairs, though TL is painting like mad two hundred yards away in the next storeroom, I am, functionally, as alone as I could ever be. Solitude and quiet are diminished qualities in the twenty-first century, and maybe I take for them what would have struck people in past centuries as a right din. Though the train doesn't actually blast its horn until it hits the first intersection a mile away, the earth shakes as it passes. The blue prong of Mount Pisgah to the south sinks under its TV tower, hawking voices speeding out from the silent stone peak; the hidden places of the forest are crossed and recrossed by streams of puffing visitors. The notion one gets from time to time on a long hike, "I am the first human ever to set foot in this place," is pure fantasy.

Nevertheless, from this iron balcony I survey a wild realm. My wedge of driveway, the overgrown pavement, the superannuated factory detritus comprise a kind of wilderness, a kind known and loved by me almost from the cradle, a relative of the trashy woods that surrounded my childhood neighborhood and which were once all the wild to me, a remnant that will increasingly stand for all the diminished province of a former empire. Not bad,

11

really, when taken on its own merits: a tragedy only when
one considers what was. I ask myself if I would be happier, wiser, better in some way if elk and bison still grazed
in the vales of the French Broad, preyed on at night by
wolves and panthers with their red eyes. I want to say "Yes,
of course," but what reasons would I give to the skeptical?
There's nothing now I have to run from to preserve my
life—except my own kind—no scratching at the walls by
night, no wild fury unleashed under the darkening eaves
of the forest. My car at forty miles an hour is more than
a match for anything I'm likely to meet. A collision with
the train fifty feet from the studio door could bring down
dinosaurs.

My studio buddies, Jack and Noah, lead me out to the
railroad tracks to see an opossum that got itself cut in half
by the train. The front half lies by the tracks; the back
half is over in the weeds, hurled there by the force of the
hit or dragged there by a scavenger. We discuss the amazing stupidity of a creature that could get itself run over by
a vehicle which, at the very least, one hears coming half a
mile off. One of us imagines that someone cruelly tied
it to the tracks, an explanation more grisly, but one that
spares the creature the onus of utter brainlessness.

Noah has decided to document with his camera the
creature's disintegration, so day after day he comes back
with reports of the opossum's progress toward oblivion.
Crows peck out its eyes. Its vertebrae lift through its back
like hills on a flat horizon. Then one day the hinder half is
gone. We discuss what might have eaten it or dragged it away.

My vote is for a fox, but then there is the question of the front half. Why does it remain, getting flatter and lighter every day, until there's not much left but formidable teeth and jaws emerging from a shrinking mouth? Jack finds the back half of another opossum in his driveway, miles away. We know it is another opossum, for it is far fresher, a new kill. But what has killed it, in a suburban neighborhood, bitten the front half and left the meatier rear, the scavenging antithesis of the creature at the tracks? These things are as great a mystery as if they were happening on another planet. What performed the butchery—dog, cat, rat, another opossum, aliens, anything at all, or nothing at all? We can't decide. We lack even the know-how to watch effectively: we would drive whatever it was away; it would come when we fell asleep.

13

Every week or so some new death lies splattered on the tracks by the studio. I am still trying to figure out how an animal can be taken by surprise by a locomotive. Perhaps, as happens sometimes with humans, these creatures have given up their lives on purpose. Perhaps, after a mere two centuries of mechanical locomotion, unused to objects traveling at that speed, they have mistaken the space between the wheels as a real opening, something that will not close again in seconds into whirling knives of steel.

DESPITE OUR TEMPORARY FASCINATION of the dead opossum, the titular organism of our studio is the groundhog. There are dozens of them up and down the river road, at least two under the foundations of every busy warehouse, odd little creatures, featureless, curious, like reddish, fuzzy, scurrying pillows. My studio mates and I were going to do a series of sentimental woodchuck paintings—like the famous blue dogs or those greeting-card cats with the enormous sad eyes—but realized there was no way to communicate that the shape was a woodchuck and not some furry, amorphous shmoo. The creature is already too droll to be joked about successfully.

Our resident groundhog dug a series of tunnels around the utility pole at the end of the studio property. We spent hours chattering, hours keeping away from our work with the groundhogs as a provocation. There were groundhog limericks, groundhog haiku, groundhog jokes, groundhog substitutions into the personnel of our favorite stories. Their mien was so contentedly humorous we imagined they were participating in the fun.

Groundhogs tend to be crepuscular, that is, active at morning and at evening, between the twilight and the dew, but they are by no means strangers to broad day. One inhabits an enormous pipe against the outside wall of the warehouse, a pipe that must have drained something significant at one time. I take apples out there, and cookies, and things I believe a woodchuck might want to eat. They are eaten, but whether by the chuck or not I do not know. As time goes by, my fuzzy friend gets less and less panicky at my approach. Now I can see a twitching brown nose sticking out of the pipe, not even bothering to run inside and hide anymore, but not yet giving me the satisfaction of full disclosure.

The groundhog is the only mammal with a holiday named after it. It is an enormous rodent, sometimes hitting fourteen pounds. My guess is it is an early Christian stand-in for the goddess Brigid, whose feast day is February 1—the day before Groundhog Day—and whose association with the solstice and the coming of spring was far more direct than the little groundhog's. Brigid arising from her cave in ancient Newgrange in Ireland on the day of the solstice does not, I suppose, have to undergo too many diminutions to become a woodchuck with tentative paws at a tunnel mouth. It lets us keep the goddess's story while pretending not to believe in the goddess anymore.

Most European nations identify themselves with eagles or lions, with some predator or creature of the air, ascendant and belligerent. I would like to visit the country which adopts the groundhog as its mascot, somewhere peaceful, some place that curls against the secrets of the earth, a little Belgium of the imagination, tables piled with cakes, the Sunday bells ringing (not too loudly), the light falling on rolling hillocks studded with salad greens.

Years ago I was hiking beside the French Broad when I came to the roadside in time to see a mother woodchuck crossing Route 191 with her three kits. I watched as a truck, veering deliberately to hit them, wiped out the babies. It was a time when I passed that spot regularly, so I was witness to what unfolded, that day and those following. Two of the babies disappeared after the first night, perhaps taken by scavengers or dragged off the pavement by their mother. The third baby lay on the roadside, though, for four more days. Every day the mother was there, too, watching over her last baby as though there were some hope for its life. She must have known it was dead. After the fourth day, the sad little body was gone, but the mother was not. For two more days she was at the roadside, lying where her baby had lain. I had thought it was grief, and surely it was, but there was something more. The mother woodchuck was bearing witness. To every driver, every boy in a pickup old as himself, to everyone who knew even a little of the story—and there must have been dozens who noticed her vigil at the roadside—her drooping sad posture broadcasting, *Look what you have done.*

OUR OWN RESIDENT WOODCHUCK did not outlast the summer. He too fell victim to the train, poor stupid thing. His elaborate system of tunnels, with their ample, fat chuck-admitting mouths, overgrown with grass, their sides softening with rain. We missed him. Maybe we got more painting done, but there was no droll, innocent life to watch from our concrete stoop at sundown.

I feel like the mother groundhog, sometimes: I follow the narrow steel slaughterhouse of the railroad tracks, kicking through the piles of bones, thin now as white hairs, whispering, *Look what you have done!*

Jack says, "There'll always be another chuck to take his place."

I think it's possible to trust too much.

16

The Anniversary

SOMETIMES IN AUTUMN when there's a cold snap after rainy weather, or in spring when cold returns after a false thaw, needles of ice stab up from the ground, fine, milky white, like the wild pelt of a subterranean beast. The ice needles are sturdier than they look; if you kneel down and touch them, they will endure until fully compromised by the warmth of your hand. That they are merely frozen water extruded through the pores of earth is a plausible explanation, but one is defeated by their regularity—like the hairs of a brush or the pattern in fabric, neither "natural" nor random—and, paradoxically, by their irregularity, by the fact that they don't appear everywhere, but just here and there, as though sown, or otherwise prepared for.

Crystalline water is a wonder that much familiarity does not dull. The Tao says, "Flow like water," but there was ice in China in Lao Tzu's day; does this imply sometimes one must "stand firm in the high places"?

There is water all through the clay around the crystals. I do not know how the water chooses which of its crystals to freeze and which to retain as liquid. I have put my tongue to the crystals. They taste of dirt, a good taste after all.

Were I a visitor from another planet, I might think that a similar—though much more haphazard—process to that of the ice crystals is the thrust of the trees out of the slopes of the mountain. Early in April their silver-gray shafts spring out of silver-gray ground as though trees and earth were made of the same substance. The deciduous giants of the Smokies stand absolutely still on a windless Palm Sunday, pillars of stone, branches of stone only occasionally now holding at their tips the subtlest mist of green. The impression of silvery uniformity is superficial, though, the kind one would form while moving too fast over unfamiliar ground. When I climb a slope to find a place to sit down and write, my heels disturb the gray forest litter enough to reveal that the earth itself is red, a rich burnt sienna, studded with multicolored shreds and fragments, sparkling with mica. The knuckles of the bloodroot rhizomes are purple and gray green. The shape I thought was discarded Styrofoam is the shell of a dead land snail, quite large, paper white and paper-thin after a winter's weathering. The gray is just a patina of winter-killed vegetation. The mineral-bejeweled organic red is the essential flesh of the land.

It's chilly. Easter is early this year. Last week there was snow. I've sought a gentle south slope to rest on, and now that I've found it, I'm almost too warm. I want to savor the feeling, though, after the long winter, and keep on my two gray jackets and my night-blue ski cap. Like the seeds beneath me, I need to bask and soak and gather strength; I want as much light, as much sheer weather, as the day is willing to give.

Striding through the forest, I notice almost nothing except the still monumentality of the great trees, the blaze of azure above them, the roll of the mountains in all directions, visible through the forest as a city of temples through immense colonnades. The visible animal life is largely comprised of soaring birds, too high and too intent on distant things to count as part of the present world. This must be what I needed to notice today: big, still things, calm things, something *massive*.

But now that I've come to rest where *small* is the ruling syllable, I see that spring already owns my little hillock. My eyes refocus on *subtle* and *near*. Cut-leaf toothwort blooms in pale pink and paler lavender. Sturdy stalks of cohosh push through the litter to uncurl, green and magenta, in the sun. One yellow violet. One anemone. A spray of stonecrop. The whitened snail shell discarded and found again as though it were a different treasure entirely. The roots of an overturned tree dry in the air at the base of my slope. I used it to pull myself up from the road. Around it stands a low cloud of bloodroot. I didn't see the crowd of them when I was climbing the log, but there they are, holding their catcher's-mitt leaves to the sun, their white stars of flowers, some blooming now, some that bloomed yesterday collapsed under their stems in a stack of petals neat as a camper's firewood. I mistook the mass of them for white light fallen through the branches.

Bloodroot is my favorite wildflower, at least until the trillium blooms a few weeks later. Trillium I can grow in my garden back home; the bloodroot keeps giving up, which but adds a twinge of the unrequited to my liking. Now that I see this patch, now that my eye knows what to look for, I notice the entire forest floor is whitened with them, a tiny snow clinging to the declivities under ridges, to the narrow ecosystems between the roots of trees. Such bounty is at once blessed and a bit daunting. I fight back the swelling conviction that I must rise up, race through the undergrowth, looking at everything, seeing every flower, nodding, acknowledging, or some precious energy of the season will be wasted. People who go around saying "Live every day as though it were your last" don't appreciate the magnitude of what that requires.

I smell a sweet, somewhat unnatural fragrance. I realize it's the smell of fabric softener from my outer jacket. The day is that calm, the air that clear.

I've carried more gear with me than usual, and the reason is, paradoxically, that I am slightly incapacitated. For one, there is the notebook I now write on. I almost never write on the trail. If you're caught at it, it looks so schoolboyish, so *poetic*. Besides, writing is a discipline of the mind and not an accident of circumstance. You are meant to keep dramatic images in mind and write them down later. Despite what some of my poetical friends say, immediacy is often triviality. What you are left with when you get home is what you probably needed to remember.

With me also is a bottle of grape juice, my old camera (which I will almost certainly not use), an inexplicable church bulletin, a book I am trying to read because in a moment of madness I agreed to do a review, a knife, a pair of gloves, a dull green satchel to carry it all in, and all this impedimenta because I can't go very fast today, anyhow, but, like a lumbering freighter, may therefore carry everything I might conceivably need.

I disabled myself to this sturdy hobble by, two days ago, learning to jump rope. Never in my youth did I jump rope. Back where I come from, males did not even conceive of it, except behind the walls of gymnasia, and then with a specific purpose in mind, some deed of force or pummeling extreme enough to masculate this basically girlish activity. A boxing champion can get away with it. But I'm a long way from youth now. I seldom worry about how things look—even if I feel I know how they look—and, being convinced of rope jumping's merits as exercise, I strode boldly into a toy store and bought a candy-striped, red-and-wheat colored rope, went home, and set to it. For half an hour I was angry and frustrated because I kept stepping on the rope, or hitting the ceiling

23

with it, or a cat. I do not catch on to complicated physical tasks quickly, and for me this matter of rope jumping was plenty complicated. But I have learned a few lessons from life, and one is that when you're up against a wall, turn and face the other way. When you're at an impasse, pass. So I went over and turned on the TV, concentrated on whatever was on, and started with the rope again as I watched. In ten seconds I was mesmerized by the program on the tube. In twenty seconds I was jumping rope. My mind having released its grip, my body had its way.

The secrets to jumping rope as I see them are: (1) Don't think about it, (2) Go a lot faster than you anticipated. The upshot of this experience was that it was so exhilarating jumping rope for the first time in my life that I kept at it for an hour, pouring sweat, struggling to breathe, counting the *whap whap whap* of the rope on the wooden floor—100, 110, 125—perfectly exhausted, perfectly happy. The next morning my *extensor digitorum longus* had turned into lumber. It is still difficult to go down stairs; on the day of the Palm Sunday hike, I had to whisper ouch under every tenth breath. More significantly, I had to use the walking stick I keep in the truck for such occasions, an object which in any other context would be called a cane.

If you're going to go as slow as I was going, do use a cane: it saves speculation.

I've walked, jogged, or cycled this road a hundred times without knowing until today that it is called Hard Times Road. I know this now because I picked up a bit of litter, which turned out to be a map someone must have gotten at the arboretum and had no more use for. Hard Times Road looks longer and harder on the map than it feels when you're on it. It is also, on a day like this, practically a thoroughfare: old men walking, families mountain biking, young men running, women running with braces of dogs running before them. I want to find this traffic annoying, but I realize I would have gone somewhere else had I wanted to be really alone. I pulled my pickup over where there were already vehicles parked in the grass. I must have wanted to share. I must have wanted that ineffable, perfect mixture of solitude and community that you can find in woods near cities.

(That, by the way, is Paradise . . . not a city, not a wilderness, but a garden . . . a park in Jerusalem.)

Hard Times Road is changed from what it was when I first knew it, and by more than the acquisition of a name. Several Halloweens ago now, a young woman named Karen Styles was brutally murdered here. She had been jogging alone when the wrong man stepped into her path. The media called it a "crime of opportunity," because neither she nor her murderer went to Bent Creek with that dark assignation in mind. Karen was tied to a tree and shot. She was so close to the road that anybody should have been able to see her, but nobody did until a hunter stumbled across her body weeks later. Karen was in the news again this season because the lawyer of the man who had been convicted of her murder found a technicality that would gain his client a new trial. There were the predictable TV interviews of her friends and family saying how unfair it was, then of the accused murderer's family, relieved that "now at last the truth can come out." We hate the media when it asks questions to which the answers are known and inevitable. Families of victims will call for justice—by which they mean retribution; families of assumed perpetrators will not be able to imagine such a deed on the part of their loved one. And the oaks lean over the bloody spot and, while stupid questions are asked and answered by anger, the stage is set for the next atrocity, which comes not out of the woods but out of the bewildered heart.

The oaks know the truth. Maybe they are the only ones.

In the fullness of time, real flaws were found in the police work, and the murderer pled guilty to involuntary manslaughter, and everyone had to let it go at that. But everything on the Hard Times Trail changed.

Now most women jog here at least in pairs, often in battalions. If they jog alone, they are usually accompanied by dogs. Big white dogs. Yet as I hobble along in the blue light, I encounter a woman jogging alone, and my reaction of dread and protective dismay probably serves to make me look suspicious myself. I realize I have a stick in my hand—my cane, my staff, my weapon. She is coming on fast and I don't know how to compose myself to look as harmless as possible. There's still that club in my hand, that cudgel, that pike. I jerk to the very edge of the road, to allow her 90 percent of it to pass by me. She does, smiling. I say "Hi!" loudly, in my best Midwestern kid voice. Wouldn't harm a fly. She says "Hi" back. I'm unable to account for my feeling of shame. I should have been smaller.

I should not have been carrying a stick. I should have been a great white malamute, loping in her wake through the spring light. I should have been here, on the road I know so well, even if I didn't know its name, those Halloweens ago when Karen Styles went jogging.

The thin snow of bloodroot curves down toward the creek. *Karen died in autumn. There were different flowers. Light hail of acorns. The bloodred dogwood leaves fluttered around her. Forest asters like blue mist.* I'm still standing transfixed in the road when the next jogger appears, a lone man in a red shirt. He is clearly unarmed. I look hard at him. I know him, a former student, Mark Something. It's all right. He's all right. It's better with Mark, whom I know, behind her. If she were to stop for any reason, he would be there in two minutes.

A few weeks earlier I had attended a conference where social issues were discussed, and one of the sessions I wandered into concerned public safety in wilderness areas and city parks. A young man was speaking of the city parks of Seattle, and how a project of undergrowth clearing was being implemented in order for people to feel—and in some cases *be*—safer in the city parks. "Two to six," I think is what it was called: brush, saplings, herbs between two feet and six feet would be cut away so vision could be unobstructed in all directions. The sunstruck gallery forest around Hard Times Road could have been an example of such an enterprise, though here the clean, open spaces were entirely natural. It was difficult to imagine how anybody could sneak up on you. Perhaps in high summer, if the killer had crowded himself right up against the road, where there is a thick line of saplings and fat shrubby weeds fighting for the light. If he had been waiting. But Karen had been jogging in October, when things were redder and browner than this gray and azure April Sunday, but not much denser. Whatever happened, she had not been caught off guard. She had to have seen it coming.

I walk ten feet more, scanning the roadside for early flowers. A stand of sticky fiddleheads, the broken skeleton of a tortoise. Far off, the gleam of the great wire fence that has been erected, so it is said, to keep the deer out of the arboretum, but which, whatever its intention, makes the woods look like a frontier between warring nations.

It occurs to me that I have almost never felt endangered anywhere. Not on the streets of New York or London or New Orleans, not in the deepest forest. I am deficient in the thoughtfulness that comes with real danger, I suppose. Three man walking toward me through the red oaks with guns in their hands make me think, "Hmmm, I didn't know it was deer season." This fearlessness may be a function of being male, or of luck, or of inattention, but whatever it is, it is a gift which I must spend some time considering.

I stop in the road and ask myself, "What *are* you afraid of?"

Of staying forever the way I am.

Of dying alone and friendless.

Of fighting with God so much that he turns away from me.

Of infection in my damaged leg.

None of those things is *here*. None of them is coming at

me out of the shadows of the forest. Or, except for the last fear, *out* of anywhere at all.

I thought for a while that I had come to the Hard Times Trail so heavily laden in order to write a poem. The detours of Karen Styles, of considerations of danger, of my concern for the solitary jogger, have so complicated things that my original intention—if that was, in fact, it—has been altered irrecoverably. If I were to write a poem now it would be one of those anniversaries the knotty poets of the seventeenth century loved so, where you take the thought of the death of someone you barely knew and use it as an occasion to reflect on life, love, destiny, eternity. But the forest is so new, so tender with fresh aspiration, that this, too, is out of the question. I feel suddenly so—well, if not wise, then burdened with wisdom, which is a wholly different thing.

The shadow the blazing light casts from me onto the road is a dark mass, warmed by too many jackets, stooped a little by the weight of a satchel and bad habits, leaning too heavily on a staff. I look old. I snap my head up, take a purposeful stride, to look like something else.

Probably the solitary jogger was not afraid of me at all. Perhaps she thought I looked sad or ridiculous. My leg is bothering me more than I thought it would. Perhaps she saw *pain*. Or middle age. Or some fool who thought you could still hobble to an April woods and gush out poems as though the world were new.

She was so young she could outrun anything, anyway.

THE GREEKS OR THE CHEROKEE would have made Karen a guardian spirit of this patch of ground—not a ghost exactly, but a kind of light where a ghost is a kind of shadow. Maybe an altar would be built, certainly a sheaf of stories would grow around her through time. A cairn. A mound. It would be nice to come back in a hundred years and see what people remember. I hope the newspaper stories and the trial accounts have crumbled to dust—or have been erased in some Internet catastrophe—by then. I hope the horror is gone and some sort of mysterious beauty remains. Fleet, dark Karen, doelike, the guardian of the autumn wood, a goddess. The Artemis of these six hills.

My thoughts turn to the murderer, and I start to ask myself the question, "What on earth would have caused someone to—" when a series of disturbing images flashes through my head. I am walking down a rocky New England shore. I am angry, disappointed, lonely, and something else, something dark and cruel, something that thinks any penalty it exacts against the unfairness of the world is just recompense. In pure frustration, I pull a periwinkle off a rock and throw it down hard. It explodes. This is somehow gratifying. I pull another off and crush it, and another and another. I think if I work hard I can clear this crescent of beach of periwinkles before high tide. I can leave the rocks bare. I can make my mark. Pulling, hurling, smashing . . .

I'm standing on the front stoop of the apartment where I used to live. I've set a bowl of milk out for the neighbors' cat—which I'm supposed to be caring for in their absence, but which has run wild, the milk a gesture of faith in her return. Slugs have come to drink the milk in the cat's stead. I watch them move slowly in the bowl for a moment, their reddish brown skin coated by slime and the blue white of the milk. Something sickens me. I can't account for it. I go to the kitchen for sea salt. I return, sprinkle the salt, and dissolve them all. For the next six nights I put milk out to draw slugs. Then sometime before morning I arrive with a box of salt. I smile inside, thinking if the slugs had any brains, if they wrote history, they would remember this. . . .

I had just moved into my house. Spring had just eased over into summer. The ants were already at work when I stepped through the door. They were scurrying across the sidewalk, up and down, zigzagging, making long diagonals, individuals pausing, doubling back in their tracks as though someone had called their name. Their activity looked frantic, random, though I knew there must be a purpose of a sort to each move they made. Some new scent, some vibration shaking through the material of the sidewalk must compel every change of direction. Only the intelligent can be distracted, and the individual members of this melee had no intelligence, though the corporation did possess a consciousness, a compelling will for the attainment of a specific goal more efficient than intelligent.

Many of the ants were carrying things, and I supposed that the rest were intending to carry them. They dragged in their mandibles dead insects, sticks, bits of larger bodies that I had no desire to identify. The throng was hunting and gathering on a gigantic level, as though the inhabitants of a whole town were to scurry into the surrounding

forests at once, hungry, alert, rapacious, hauling back anything that failed to move out of the way.

Ant City lay under my front terrace somewhere. Its activity went on through my lawn and perhaps the adjacent
lawns, but I only saw it when the ants crossed porch steps
and the sidewalk. If their numbers in the grass were pro-
portionate to their numbers on the concrete, there were
horrifying myriads of them.

But I think that they preferred the cement and that
most of them at a given time would be gathered there,
where they could be seen and appropriately honored
for their prodigiousness. Whatever danger accrued from
being in the open like that was compensated by speed of
transport and ease of carrying, a wide highway where you
don't have to climb stalks and batter through baffles every
inch of the way. It wasn't possible for a whole lawn to be
boiling with like proportion of such rapacious, consum-
ing life; they must have congregated on the cement on
purpose, as we would on a beach between a forest and an
impassable sea.

I sit on the porch eating lunch and watching the ants.
I drop crumbs to them, a manna-scattering god. Com-
pared to the tidbits they glean from the grass, my gifts are
enormous—whole turkeys, picnics, sides of cows. I want
the gratification of seeing them take my offerings, so if
they are slow to discover the food, I pick one of them up
and drop it right down on the crumb. This must be done
quickly and carefully, for they bite without regard to your
motivation. They hoist the crumb up over their backs, and

I try to watch where they take it, wondering if I can find the Ant Citadel. But there are too many of them crossing and scurrying too many ways, and trying to follow one is a little nauseating. Nor do they seem to be going all in one direction. Some of the successful hunters seem to be heading one way, others another, when one would expect them all to be aiming for a central larder. It crosses my mind that they do not know where they are going, that they cross and recross with their gargantuan burdens until accidentally stumbling upon something familiar, or until they die of exhaustion, to be picked up and carried by one identical to themselves, with the same stupid, purposeless implacability.

I spend a long time watching the ants, although, if the truth be told, I hate them. The reason for my hatred is not entirely clear, though I think it has something to do with energy without soul, with victory going to them who can derive from it neither wisdom nor pleasure. If I were to die undiscovered in the lawn, they would cut me into tiny pieces and haul me away without regard for what I was, without regard even for my regard of them.

Two things happened one day that summer, which led to an outcome that I still cannot fully explain. The first was a news report of a little girl horribly disfigured by denatured alcohol, which burns with such withering pure heat that it is invisible. I forget how she caught on fire, but the image from the story that stuck with me was of the girl running and screaming and onlookers seeing her features darkening and crumbling, but unable to tell what was the

33

matter until it was too late. As far as they could see, she was screaming in impalpable agony and clawing at empty air.

The second incident was more personal and more trivial. I was sitting on my front steps eating cake. My niece had baked the cake as one of her first culinary efforts and shipped it between states to her favorite uncle, who was damn well going to consume it, every morsel, for the sake of the affection that went into the making. Five feet beyond the step I sat on, the ants were swarming. There were hills, mounds, a vast seething plain of red-brown bodies, scurrying and horrible. For a moment I tried to imagine why they were swarming on this particular day, but exploration of the psychology of the soulless is a long, spiral tunnel, at the end of which is darkness. Still, I could not look away. There were simply too many of them. Had they been one animal as they were one will, they would have been the size of a dog, a bad dog, a threat.

Some atmospheric condition made the day too muggy and sticky to be inside and at the same time made the swarm irritable and aggressive, so that as I sat on the steps eating cake—a position and an activity normally safe, even considering the predators in the grass—I was bitten again and again. Long spiraling detachments of ants came off the central swarm, like the arms of galaxies swirling from the center. The crumbs I dropped were instantly overwhelmed by dark brown bodies, but instead of thanks I was given painful nips. Sometimes the sting didn't end when I brushed the biter away, for if I brushed too hard, I would separate the ant from its mandibles, which would stay imbedded in the flesh, gnawing and injecting formic acid after the creature whose defense it was lay dead.

As the seconds went by, this treatment made me more and more angry. It was my porch, my steps, my cake. The ants were too stupid to associate the blessed rain of cake crumbs with their victim and far too dim to appreciate the loving labor of my niece. They found, lifted, toted the crumbs as though they were ordinary dead bugs, as though they were nothing. They bit the source as though it would hurry away and leave its benefit behind, the blessing of a god without the god. They were dumb mouths, tiny walking appetites, heedless.

There were too many. Too stupid.

I hated them.

I thought of the burned girl and I thought of my niece at the oven with her cake; I thought of my swatting at the tiny fires their skirmishes left in my legs. I thought of the denatured alcohol sitting under the sink like a blade in a sheath. When I purchased it, the conscious need was for refinishing furniture, but at that instant I realized I had not bought it—would not have thought to buy it—until after I'd read of the burning girl. There are motivations it does not pay to scrutinize too closely.

I pulled the white can out of the dark. I got a book of matches. I walked outside. I poured the alcohol in a wide circle around the main swarm of the ants on the sidewalk. I didn't want them to die right off from contact with the alcohol. I wanted them to *know* they were dying. That they were being called to account. I wanted them to wither in the center of a ring of fire. I put the can carefully to one side, so it wouldn't explode. I lit a match and threw it on the ring of alcohol.

Just as the news story of the burned girl suggested, there was nothing at first. I had to sit down on the porch steps to get a brighter background behind the burning place, against which the heat waves could be seen rippling and dancing. I could see tiny brown bodies blackening and shriveling, but, because of the turbulence of the fire, they kept on jerking as though they were alive. Invisible fire withered the ends of the grasses, crept out into the lawn, blackening and destroying while remaining itself all but undetectable. I wanted to throw more alcohol on the flames, to make it spread until it lit the ants scurrying into the grass, until agonized bodies brought the conflagration to the nest, to the citadel, and I could see it withering away as well. I would have done it had not the image entered my head of a finger of fire climbing the tossed alcohol, back to the source, catching it, setting me aflame with the ants, me running in inarticulate agony, withering and scream-ing while nobody knew exactly what was wrong.

The fire lasted longer than I expected. I was afraid it would begin to consume the lawn. If the fire trucks had to be called, how would I explain it? Then the heat ripples began to fall from the air. What looked like dark sand spread over the sidewalk, but it was the innumerable dead bodies of the army of the ants. They shifted and disappeared when the wind blew. They were made nothing. Single ants came out of the grass wilderness, prowling among the bodies of

their kin. What were they thinking? That they were thinking nothing at all I refused to entertain. I wanted there
to be wisdom, warning, terror. I wanted the day to have
consequence. Even a monster would not want to waste all
that pain. I did not feel like a monster. I felt, fleetingly,
like a god.

The sentence at the tip of my tongue concerning Karen
Styles, that one beginning, "What on earth could have
caused someone to—" never got finished. Like Job, I sat
back upon the dung heap and shut my mouth. Making
high declarations like "Nothing human is foreign to me,"
we must be prepared for the world to catch us in our
own boast; we must mean it, all of it. The Greeks, or
the Cherokees, or the local newspaper would have had a
name for me, too, had I been caught at the annihilation
of my neighbors, had something gone wrong with the fire.
That it was just mollusks and myrmidons I tortured is not
the point.

Then it occurred to me. Karen Styles was already a
spirit in the dappled light. She was hovering in the wild
places, already the Artemis of the near hills, guarding, giving warning, maybe not of somebody *out there,* but of somebody *in here.*

Grab the walking stick a little harder. Bend to the road.
Go on.

Cruising Princeton

I TELL PEOPLE I don't go on expeditions into the wilderness to watch exotic animals, but maybe I do. Maybe I simply haven't taken time to consider what I mean by "wilderness" and "animal." Of course, we are all animals, as well as angels, and when I watch the bodies of men, I watch the bodies of animals. But observing them is complicated, for they are bodies that are capable of knowing they are being watched, bodies whose captured spirit is capable of watching back, judging with the same judgment. I do go on expeditions into the wilderness. I close the car door, turn the key in the ignition.

On this occasion I am traveling north. My father lives in Akron, Ohio, and I must have been driving through the West Virginia mountains to visit him. I got a late start. It's afternoon, with three or four hours of plain light left to me. When I see the sign for Princeton, West Virginia, I decide to pull over.

Princeton is the sort of place one normally passes through, as a naturalist passes a vacant lot on his way to a rainforest. In our travels as a family long ago, Father would make us stop at indistinguishable little hamlets in order to get the local flavor, and maybe because I wanted to think of my own journeys as direct, swift, and purposeful, I had half-unconsciously scorned this practice. But I am older now, freer to explore what would have looked once like spiritual compromise. Plus, father was right. Discoveries are made on the way. Think of Saul of Tarsus: he imagined that nothing much was going to happen until he finally got to Damascus.

Check in at the motel.

Test the TV in case the area is as bare of incident as it seems from the interstate. Cable. Saved.

Grab a salad at the Western Steer. I have come to the watering hole and all the creatures are assembled with me. Frosted-haired women bellow at toddlers. Stubble-faced fathers cut meat, lecture, snap at fussy toddlers. Married couples gaze past each other out the sunset-stricken windows. The Western Steer that evening is a bad place for a single person, weighed down as it is by the heft of gobbling families.

The solitary hunters in nature are at a disadvantage. Like the leopard, these loners might be fierce and beautiful, but most of what they do must be done in stealth.

Who is that? they will think, looking toward my booth at the window. No one will know. If they would just look away and go on chowing down, that would be all right, but my portable insecurities make me think they will keep on looking until they make some guesses, and whether I fear right guesses or wrong ones more is difficult to tell.

I am a hunter. Look to your old ones and your children.

The checkout woman looks as though she were sent from Central Casting, her ash-blond beehive mounting over a pink uniform, name tag—Phyllis—secured by a pink plastic corsage, lipstick-darkened cigarette balanced on the top of the cash register with the burning end pointing, considerately, away from the feeding families. The effect, however, is not droll, but rather sibylline. There is something mysterious, something knowing about her. I ask where "downtown" is, and she points, blowing air between her layers of lipstick, as though she were exhaling a drag of her Camel.

She says, "You won't find what you're looking for there." I smile and shrug. I think I will.

Phyllis short changes me. I'm too embarrassed to say anything . . . it's only a buck or so, and maybe this is a test the locals put strangers to . . . but before I reach the door, Phyllis is upon me, whooping her apologies, waving the dollar in the air, so our exchange becomes a public event.

41

I drive on past the restaurant to the Princeton "down-town," a real if tiny urban area rising in contrast to the straggle of abandoned motels and bare fields around it. I park on the street and walk. I wish I had dressed for a Sunday night. Likely I had forgotten it was a Sunday night. The colors are wrong; the display will not read right, either to prospective mates or foreseeable enemies. They will not know why I am here. This could be dangerous. It could be merely lonely.

The streets of Princeton, West Virginia, are alive, teem-ing, an uncommon thing in the era of malls. Like other last-quarter-of-the-twentieth-century downtowns, it's scruffy and gap-toothed. Halfway houses and Evangelical churches stand where theaters once disgorged their happy crowds. Dusty windows open onto vacant rooms. Airborne trash tangles in the unpruned shrubbery. But what hap-pens on the streets has nothing to do with their state of repair. There is vibrancy and expectation. The citizens of Princeton at their evening constitutionals are like a festal procession passing through a ruined cathedral.

The creatures move on the plain, their eyes wide, nostrils flaring. Some are afraid. Some are on the hunt. Some watch.

Two basic sorts of people were at large. First were Christians going to Sunday evening service in the variety of storefront evangelical hot spots. Several conventional church buildings studded the downtown area, but these seemed to be closed or operating at a level of intensity completely obscured by the gospel storefronts.

The meeting goers paused in their conversations on the sidewalk when I appeared. They greeted me from behind starched pastel dresses and hot black suits. I hoped someone would invite me in. I would have gone. But maybe my fatigues, black T-shirt, and mirror sunglasses made them think I had come looking for other things. The colors are wrong. The display won't read. I listened as I passed them, gathered in the lingering Sunday afternoon twilight before services began. They talked of family and money. People repeated what had just been said, to show how intensely they had been listening. They amened and yes lorded. When it was time for the service to start, they put their hands on the centers of their friends' backs, to guide each other in.

I have never done that. The gesture would be awkward, unconvincing. They would know I wasn't one of them.

The second type of people on the street were teenagers prowling in a hundred different kinds of vehicles— "cruising" as one sees mostly in nostalgic movies now, shouting to one another and to the occasional passerby on the sidewalk, or to stationary teenagers gathered in vacant lots like celebrities in a parade viewing stand. A boy in a truck equipped with a loudspeaker called me "dude" three times before I looked at him. I thought he was going to mock me for some trespass only an outsider would commit, but when I finally acknowledged him he smiled and asked for the time. He didn't want the time. He wanted contact, for himself and for me. He wanted to welcome me to the sweet dishevelment.

There were girls with blond hair tousled as though all had shampooed at once and hit the street hair still wet. Boys with caps pulled low and sleeves rolled high, tanned from whatever it was they did all day. They longed for each other, but understood that something had to precede the simple attainment, some ceremony, some delicious and flashy postponement. I longed for them, too, in a sort of abstract way—longed for the time they inhabit, for the innocence with which they were able to let their desires be known. The very abstraction of my own desire was a disappointment to me.

I wanted to watch. This time merely to watch. To be invisible and unmarked. I had come up from the valleys into the hills. Maybe I was sleeker and stronger, maybe I wasn't. If the test came, I would be ready.

The lower end of the Princeton main street, where it dead-ends into the railroad tracks, is a ghost town of derelict buildings, of roofless factories and ruined warehouses, of people leaning from the windows of the apartments still habitable, talking in soft voices while their printed curtains flutter in the wind.

I enter a shotgun grocery run by, plainly, two gay men—if the colors are right, if I have read the display. They stand when they see me, as though expecting trouble. I have, after all, dressed like a hoodlum. They're talking about a memorable night spent in Roanoke. They're dishing people unknown to me. I stalk past them to the cooler, select the one thing they seem to have in abundance:

chocolate milk. The expiration date is today; I decide to take my chances.

"Will that be cash?" one says.

I chuckle. "Do people around here often use credit cards to pay for a chocolate milk?"

"Food stamps," he answers. I suddenly feel crude and luxurious. I stand on the street, swilling my milk, afraid I'll look ridiculous if I drink and walk at the same time, a waif chugging chocolate amid the ruins.

Across from a derelict factory stood yet another storefront church, more exposed to the street than those uptown. Inside, people wailed and swayed on the balls of their feet, one exceptionally beautiful and well-dressed young woman was having hands laid on her forehead by a sweating elder. I crossed the street to pass as close as possible. I wondered if I dared to go in, finally deciding that curiosity was an inappropriate motive for the entering of a holy place.

On the sidewalk before the church were a boy of twelve or thirteen and a girl a few years younger. The girl was skinny, energetic, straightforward. The boy was bespectacled, overweight, trapped in a fancy suit a size too small for him. Sometimes he stood in the doorway looking in. Sometimes he hid just past the outside door frame, as though theatrically avoiding the glance of somebody within. He was plainly in a paroxysm of uncertainty. Perhaps he was deciding whether he belonged to the ceremony or not. The young male at the edge of the pride, not knowing if he were still welcome or if it were time to strike out on his own. He looked intelligent, out of place, mortified. He looked, in fact, like me at that age. I felt a tenderness toward him that must be like the tenderness of fathers who see what lies ahead for their sons and can do nothing. He paced the hot street.

As I strolled by, oozing secularity, his allegiance firmed for a moment, and he began to sing a gospel hymn, in a voice strong, deep for a child, and very beautiful. I smiled. I wanted to speak, but it would have interrupted his song. We watched each other until the street bent. I wanted to know whether he sang for me or against me, or without any thought of me at all. I have a feeling it was defense against my approach, but perhaps it was an invitation, an open door.

I wish I'd paused to see whether he had entered the storefront or gone home at last. I voted for home. The savannahs are wide. There are other places rich in opportunity.

Yellow evening light had shaded into purple when I came up again to the main drag. I was the only walker left on the sidewalks. The cars kept on, though. I watched the cruisers until it was long past dark, when only their headlights revealed their passage, and one must select, if one wished to select at all, by faith.

I mention sometimes that I spent a night in Princeton, West Virginia. On purpose. I expect people to take it the same way as if I had said, "I have just returned from an expedition to Belize," but they don't. They say, "Oh, do you know someone there?" and I've almost answered yes before I remember my coming as a stranger, leaving as a stranger, my mind filled with faces and voices never to be known again, people who might remember me—if at all—as background in a dream, an attendant desperado fit to swell the progress of the night street.

The colors were almost right. A family resemblance, a difficult dialect . . . We almost read the signs. It almost happened. One of them walked on and disappeared into the night. One spat his longing out as song.

Nine Flames of Red

ROLLING THUNDER BEFORE DAWN; the moon behind the
bunched clouds is trembling.

My roses are lasting deep into November. Two are red.
Different reds, they are, though the difference is difficult
to describe: one a shade purpler, as though it were never
quite out of twilight, the other with a blush of pink, like a
courtesan reddened with a memory of youth. One is gold,
which pinks and scarlets as it matures until it is, at one
point, nearly all the colors a rose can be. Except white. All
white is waiting in the north.

When I saw the first deep frosts had not killed them, I

went out to tend them with renewed tenderness. I rubbed
the aphids off their buds with the tips of my fingers. I
worked the rose food into the soil with a kitchen spoon,
imagining they might know the difference in touch between
that and the ordinary—the garden variety, one would say—
trowel. They are lovelier than they ever were in the summer. Maybe it was too hot then. Maybe now their insect
adversaries are stunned by the chill.

I don't remember what flower was first in the spring.
One prizes endurance beyond precocity, especially as one
passes into the company of those who have endured.

I send my friends e-mail messages about the progress
of my garden, especially of my roses. It left them with the
impression, I think, that I was concerned with nothing else.
I felt no urgency in correcting that notion. People obsessed
with their gardens have probably caused the least suffering
in the world of any category of men.

I think about the plants because they have never struck
me as being merely *plants*, even as I seldom think of my
cats as merely *animals*. There is more to everything than the
classifiers want to bother with. There is more to everything
than meets the eye. If plants have moods—I think they
do—the mood my roses are in is exuberant defiance. It is
Veterans Day and they are a wall of perfumes.

When I first conceived the notion of a garden—after
living a student's life and then an artist's life of rent-
als with no yards—I went to my friend Michael, a locally
renowned rose man, for advice on roses. His unexpected

response was a grave expression and the observation, "Roses aren't for you." He later repented and sent me Web pages concerned with roses—simple roses, hardy roses, that an idiot can't kill—but the impression was left, the damage was done. Roses were not for me. Where had he gotten that idea? What history between me and the roses did he divine to which I was oblivious? The comment interested me because I wanted to know how and from what perception it had arisen, but I am too embarrassed actually to ask. The fact is that for several years the only rose in my garden was a miniature red used once as a prop in a play and later planted against the front stairs. It staunchly refused to die. Was it the case that all the nursery roses held their leaves before them crying "No! No!" when I strolled by?

But now, I have my roses, roses holding on to the brink of Thanksgiving, red and gold, and the gold itself turning to red. I stand with my feet in the dirt and stare at them. I walk around them in different lights. I look out every morning after the radio has talked of a "hard frost" and "freeze warnings" to see if they're black and gone, but they're not.

After the first such warning, I rushed into the garden and cut the blossoms, red and red and gold, and put them in a vase to preserve them inside for a while longer. I never used to pick my flowers, never used to put them into vases, so one knew that cutting them finally was a gesture of desperation. The next morning, the buds I left were a little fuller, glowing a little deeper from the rub of cold. And inside, the plucked ones shed their petals day by day onto the mantel. Even if the roses die inside, their petals must be gathered up and scattered back onto the garden.

After I developed the habit of picking flowers and bringing them inside, there was the problem of what to do with them when they faded. The trash can was out. The solution came to be the shady cave behind my rhododendron shrubs. Vases full of lilies, of red and gold and white roses fall into the darkness behind the rhododendrons. It must be the most exquisite soil in the world now, fed by the fine dust of roses.

IT IS NOW THE SUMMER after the winter in which the preceding was written. I have a fence of roses between me and the house next door. I have a front slope bristling with white and pink ground-cover roses. I cut roses all the time and put them in my house, convinced finally of the truth that the more the flowers are cut, the more new flowers come behind. Besides, it's a way to keep ahead of the beetles. On some days it's the perfume of the roses in my house, on some days that of the big red and gold lilies I planted everywhere some ground was left. Big flowers, the horses of the flowers. Jugs and punch bowls to arrange them in. I move the vase of roses or of lilies into my bedroom at night, always to have them with me. I eye the neighbor's old dark spruces, wondering what would bring them down, that I might have more light in the front yard. I regret that the sweet gum in my backyard is so beautiful. Otherwise, it could be removed, and the rose light flood

in from the south and east. I am not proud of this attitude. It is greed, a vice like any other.

MY RELATIONSHIP WITH GARDENS becomes, in places,
complex. Some of my earliest memories are of my father's
garden on Goodview Avenue in Akron, Ohio, terraced and
alive with jumbles of sunstruck flowers, cosmos, gladi-
ola, sunflowers I thought I could almost climb. I inher-
ited my father's propensity for big, horsey blooms with
stalks that can draw blood. The other garden I knew well
was Grandmother's garden, my mother's mother's garden, shadier and subtler, favoring bushy old-fashioned
bloomers like peony and bleeding heart. People do not
remember that I was a wildly enthusiastic gardener as a
child. They do not remember because that sweet time was
followed by years in which I refused to acknowledge either
yard or the garden, because in order to function there I
would have to obey rather than create. People who might
remember my initial enthusiasm would not know what
caused the change, but I do. From time to time I asked for
plots, carved from the coarse Ohio grass, in which I might
grow things, and my father obliged me, but there almost
always followed a war that neither of us understood fully.

Part of it was simply that I was interested in flowers and
my father assumed it was a man's place to grow vegetables.
That sounds quaint and absurd, but anything unexamined
can assume vast proportions, and an issue such as this,
which would be blown away by a breath if ever brought into
the open, hovered for a decade like a dark wall between

53

father and son. That I preferred flowers *because* he preferred vegetables would be a superficial and probably incorrect analysis, but in some ways it is easier to go with than the truth. The truth is I could hear the voices of the flowers and could not, reliably, hear the voices of the vegetables. Today I have eggplant and horseradish aging among my energetic roses. I planted them because I could hear them. Give me a while to think about it before you ask why.

There was a flower show every year at Betty Jane Elementary School, and one year my father made an arrangement for me, very masculine twigs of flowerless bushes in a big squat green Depression vase. The fact is that the arrangement was stylish and elegant and would have won a prize in a more sophisticated venue, but I was struck even then by the bloomlessness of it. It was not just a flower show entry; it was a lecture, and a persuasive one. Mother made my sister an arrangement of blazing autumn flowers, mostly electric orange zinnias, in a sky-blue vase in the shape of a donkey pulling a cart. My sister won a ribbon. I didn't. I wonder if my father knew how long I pondered that lesson, without ever exactly knowing what it was. Set yourself up for defeat? Let the girls carry the flowers? The other side of the lesson was that I knew my father was right. If someone has a flower show, you don't necessarily have to bring the same jug of glads everyone else is bringing. I resented my father and wanted to champion him simultaneously in such a confusion of impulses that I never again responded to the call for flower show entries. This is called "growing up."

Though father kept his vegetable garden until recently, the flowers diminished year by year—narrowing
down at last to a patch of tulips, which seemed, somehow,
statutory for a suburban front yard in Ohio, or perhaps
uniquely gender-free—and those which remained were
mostly planted by me and dwelt in constant threat from
the mower. The double hollyhocks I'd smuggled in as seeds
from a place we'd visited in California, the nicotiana
around the fish pond, the great pink Hawaiian hibiscus
I'd gotten as a prize in a contest, one by one became the
focus of unaccountable paternal ire and one by one fell to
the whirling metal blades.

I think that part of the phasing out of flowers was
my father's own developing sense of gender. Part of it was
deeper and older, was in fact a question of territory and
how to keep it free of encroachment, even by an heir. I
was not supposed to make my own statement in his yard;
I was, instead, supposed to mow and trim to his liking
so that his landscaping statements would have an air of
family unanimity. You can bet this did not happen. You
can imagine the hours of squabbling, the orders given and
ignored, the threats and sulking, neither of us precisely
clear on what the quarrel was about.

I lived on a commune north of Baltimore for a while,
and once, when a cardinal flower had sprung up in the
middle of the vegetable garden, Dick Falkenstein, the head
gardener, made all the furrows bend at that place, so the
cardinal flower could live out its life, a red blaze at the
head of a bent field of soybeans. That was a lesson one can

ponder for a lifetime, but part of the lesson is "allow it all." It is a lesson—out of so many ignored—I have learned. Any volunteers in my garden are allowed, anything vaguely flowery. Wild indigo came up this year, and early in spring a single white trillium. I have lived here for twelve years, and I swear that trillium never bloomed before.

When I finally bought my own house with my own bit of land attached to it, I discovered that, after twenty years of not so much as sinking a spade into the earth, I was once again an avid gardener. I'd learned the lesson: don't try to define an environment that's not your own. If a man loves the rolling flat grass of the suburbs, don't provoke him with spears of hollyhocks and interrupting patches of nasturtium. If a man has drawn back into the comforting roughness of bark and foliage, don't confuse an already difficult issue by prancing about with blossoms in your hand.

When it came time to choose my garden, I felt my mind turning down two roads, back to the gardens I remembered from my extreme childhood, my grandmother's, my father's before his vision of things changed, and out to the deep forest that I loved, and the testimony of which the abundant shade of my little property made practical. I scoured the Internet nurseries for bloodroot, jack-in-the-pulpit, foxglove, trillium, wild ginger, as many exotic ferns as I thought would fit.

I took counsel with my memory, until certain images from vanished gardens had solidified again in my mind: bleeding heart, chaotic perfumed peonies, lilac, crocus, blue hydrangea big as a child's head, magenta four-o'clocks, great spears of lupine, the low succulent my grandmother called cat-and-kittens. As I began haunting Saturday morning farmers' markets and receiving—as if by telepathic urging—commercial garden catalogs, the spectrum grew to include plants that no one in my family had ever kept.

Flowers, too, are a type of custom, a sociology lesson in themselves; Mr. Fulmer next door to my grandparents grew roses; Mr. Johnson across the street grew iris; Grandmother grew hydrangeas and peonies, and it seemed to me then that these were acknowledged alternatives, mutually exclusive, a sort of political alignment that could be mixed or defied only at peril. An iris in Mr. Fulmer's garden would have caused sleepless nights and midnight phone calls. My grandparents were Irish and, oddly, anti-labor union. Would one have been able to read that in their front yard of a May morning? Did their peonies wither when the placards from the rubber-plant strikers marched down Hampton Road?

As so much time had passed since I had last puttered in a garden, and in so many ways I had broken with family tradition already, I felt free to interlope on all sides. My own culture is eccentric but definite, like the biota of an atoll out alone in the middle of the sea. I felt the ancient garden imperatives stretched and broken for me, ready to be remade. I would be a United Nations, a melting pot of horticulture. It would be a big, gaudy mess, and I would love it. I'll plant everything I want and see what wants me.

Into the dirt around my house went crown imperial, like a halo of orange fire; yellow iris; not only my father's pink bleeding heart, but white, and a pale yellow climbing variety, delicate but unkillable; every poppy I could lay my hands on, the deepest red or the most solar orange; gold lupine; as much of the tribe of hollyhock as I could find— maybe I was haunted by the ghosts of the plants I could not save from my father's mower: black—which unless the sun is directly behind really is black; red, reddish, pink, white, big yellow perennials from the steppes of Russia; a petite lavender that the catalog said was an "heirloom" from old gardens, welcome now to mine. I thought I hated daffodils, but into the ground went a throng of bulbs because they were meant to be green when they bloomed and were called "Saint Patrick." We'll see in March.

I find a coffee can of catnip plants at the farmers' market over behind Asheville Pizza and Brewing. I bring it home and set the seedlings in a sunny spot. When I walk out onto the porch two hours later, the neighbors' cat, Toonses, a black scamp, is rolling in the plants in feline delight. My spike of anger rises and subsides within seconds. The plants were catnip, after all—what else should he do? My cats never leave the house, so it is Toonses who is at my elbow when I'm gardening, stalking the routed bugs, rolling around in the fresh dirt, pawing at my elbow as it goes in and out over my work. It is Toonses who lies under the cool of the hollyhock stalks in summer like a panther at ease amid the trees of a forest. "All right," I hear myself saying, "you're welcome." Toonses repays me by coming up silently in the dark when I am fussing with my keys, rubbing the backs of my legs, so that there is a moment of blind panic until the inner voice whispers, "Just a cat." Toonses repays me by watching the birds at my feeder from a polite distance, never leaping, never stalking, leaving that to my own housebound hunters, quivering and purring with their wet noses against the picture window.

I developed of late a hunger for red. Among the poppies wave forty lilies, all of them shades of red, spotted or striped or throated dramatically with gold. Into the shady backyard went foxglove and crimson wake-robin and cobra lilies—alabaster-throated—long-tongued Oriental relatives of the woodland jack-in-the-pulpit. The sun-blasted slope of the front terrace hosts daylilies (red, orange, gold), butterfly bush, bee balm, blue alyssum, pink echinacea, giant asters that form a blue mist at stalk tops in the autumn. There is too much; the effect is chaos, but I don't care. I'm waiting for the plants to sort themselves out, for those that wish to stay to stay, and those that would rather not to let their spirits pass into the air.

"Spirits" is not meant to be poetic. I realize I do not normally talk to other gardeners, so I don't know if they perceive their flowers as spirits. The embarrassing vocabulary of the New Age is in this matter almost impossible to avoid. When I lived on that commune in the '70s, the commune of the cardinal flower, all the talk of the "devas of the bean plants" made me cringe, but now the same perception comes independently to my heart, inclining me to the same vocabulary. There is a vibrancy and will—in the spears of iris pushing through the barely thawed soil, in the rough salad of foxglove and hollyhock leaves that don't fade in deepest winter—something more than botanical. I feel like the old wives of legend, hobbling between my rows of blossoms, listening to them for hints of their powers and virtues.

I do check the field guides before I actually eat any-thing. A tisane of foxglove simply would not do.

When it warms up again, I will go out and spade up more garden, for the seeds and bulbs a winter's gleaning of the eBay gardening section won me. Some flowers I never heard of. Some flowers I have loved since childhood and never found before. What an age this is! Turkish pop-pies . . . Russian hollyhocks . . . Dutch iris . . . Tennessee jack-in-the-pulpit . . . Martian crown imperial . . .

Most of the front yard, where there is sun, is already eaten up, but what use have I for grass? I look sometimes at the giant sweet gum that shades most of the backyard, and though I would never touch it, I wonder how long it has left of its natural life. The blast of sun that would come with its passing might shock the ferns and the cobra lilies and the lilies-of-the-valley, so I let things be. The neighbor's spruces are very old and perched precariously on a slope. A hard winter, ice, and a hard wind, and they might tip right over into the street. That would be too bad, but thirty square feet of my land would be opened to the light.

The first thing I did after the rolling dawn thunder was check my roses. Out in the gray world, under the gray rain: nine flames of red, seven of gold. The rain on them is hanging jewels. Ruby. Golden sapphire. I would gather and keep. It is greed, a vice like any other, except it requires no theft, encourages abundance sown on all sides, for all.

FOR THE SAKE OF THE BLOSSOMS running wild in Connemara, I bought foxglove seedlings from a lady at the farmers' market. Fallow last year, blooming this one, they turn out to bear cornets of ivory magenta, blood-speckled within, spike upon spike, more than I remember, as if they meant to push out of my little sweet-gum shaded terrace and throng the world.

It's not so early in the morning as I wish, and here I stand, in black silk pants remaining from the revelries of last night, watering my foxgloves. The hose puts drops of topaz on the spikes of—it appears now—silk, blood, and orchid. The hose wets the silk and pushes it into the contours of my body. I am reminded how everything has its proper symbol and its sign. I move among the lances of the flowers, black of my apparel the only black, white of my body the only white, where everything else is mottle and dapple. I touch my tongue to the drops as they lie on the blossoms. The foxgloves are poison, of course; this is part of the thrill. I shut my eyes against the light and the flood of jewels from the mouth of the hose, against the ghost of hangover. Suddenly, I am not here. I am in Connemara, where the spears of the foxgloves run rank on rank from the blue hills to the steel gray sea. Such a sob tears from my throat. Only a hummingbird is there to hear. I'm glad. I have no words of explanation, and the hummingbird does not ask. He waits for the artificial rain to stop, then darts into the red heart of the flower.

Troubadours

SEPTEMBER.

That high, throbbing, mechanical sound in the air throughout the morning hours could be taken for construction on the next block, or for one of those internal combustion vacuum juggernauts used for sweeping supermarket parking lots. The sound changed as it moved closer. It changed again as it moved away, dopplering across the hills with stately slowness. I'm told it's employed as the sound of warrior insects in monster movies. There's no reason not to believe it. It is in fact the voice of an army, a host, not of men but of the periodical cicada.

"Voice" is not accurate. It is the creature scraping itself, scraping the waxy chitin of its body, a mechanical sound rather than a vocal one.

The center of the din was once north and east of Asheville. It has moved along the trees toward the center of town, then out again into the forests along the highways to the south and west. It's thin and silvery close up, oddly inorganic, like the jangling of an infinity of high silver bells. The effect is physical; the sound presses on the chest like waves of an incoming tide. I imagine the sheer force of sound waves emanating from so many bodies, however tiny.

The local newspaper, never having come to grips with actual *news,* reports on the cicadas daily. The sensitive and the irritable phone the police to ask if anything can be done. The paper interviews people who claim they shout as a matter of course to be heard over the noise, who say that they lie sleepless through the singing nights, that the dog is losing its hair, that the grass is withering. I didn't hear the cicadas until someone pointed them out. I didn't hear the neighbors' dogs after the first night. I don't hear the phone unless I am lonely and wanting a call.

Few of the discomfited are comforted when they learn that the source of the noise is very beautiful: the periodical cicada, which appears every seventeen years in the north, every thirteen or so in the south, is black and crystal and viridian and chrysoprase. Women would wear its image as a jewel in more natural times. There are cicadas every summer, of course, providing the buzzing music of sultry nights, but they are not the same animal as this now throng-ing the treetops. Those others are an everyday creature, big, but dull and without personal assertiveness. Above all, there are never so many of them. These now singing in the trees are ruby eyed, golden winged, jet-and-golden bod-ied, huge and musical. They are the size of hummingbirds and fly with the whirring deliberation of windup toys.

A locally noted preacher said in a TV interview that, yes indeed, these are the locusts incited by God in his ven-geance in times past, and though he wouldn't say they were sent as a sign and judgment on our town just yet, his eyes and his voice lifted so as to intimate it is a possibility worth worrying about. His sources are not quite, in this matter, inerrant. The insects are called the seventeen-year locust, but have nothing to do with the Bible's flying plague, which were grasshoppers and, in evolutionary terms, tyros. Our cicadas arose in the Permian and, almost alone of that dis-tant flowering of life, survive. They sang from tree ferns when the grandmothers of the dinosaurs pawed in streams flowing from the spanking new Appalachians. They will leave the ends of branches brown and withered where they lay their eggs, but they can hardly be called a plague. Like the seraphim, their effect is almost entirely musical.

They live in secret for as long as seventeen years, suck-ing juice from the roots of trees. Suddenly, on some pri-vate signal, they climb into the light. They shed their drab grub skins and emerge in the colors of jewels. Once they emerge they are possessed of a radiant singleness of pur-pose: they mate and sing. Nothing else. When they are

finished with these activities, they flutter to the ground
and die, buzzing like wounded frogs, or are devoured by
cats, ants, mice, crunched under the tires of bicycles. In
the millions they die a serene, if graphic, death after a
season of fulfillment.

I am given to understand that the metamorphosis of a
creature reflects its evolution—that dragonflies once were
what their larvae are now, voracious pond creatures, no
more fit for the air than the mud they crawl in; that the
cicada once was utterly its dark nymph in the dark earth,
sucking the juices of a hidden world. What I want to know
is, how were they summoned into shining air? How did it
cross their unimaginable little minds even to commence
such a journey? Yes, I know how it's supposed to work,
but all the time there has been since the beginning of
time should not be enough to turn the one thing into
the other.

Since the cicadas began this year, they reminded me of
something. This morning I thought of what: certain men
and women, artists, mystics, seers, countertenors, poets,
pastry cooks, who are gorgeous in certain impractical ways,
unmistakable for anything but themselves, loud, often
barren in a biological sense, personally ephemeral if per-
sistent as a class, widely but not universally reviled, fixed
on two things alone: love and song.

I'll be deep into middle age when the cicadas swarm
again. Barring the diseases that come with bad habits and
vocational dangers, my family is long-lived. I could see the
cicadas twice more. Thrice, even. Three more visitations in

this life. I saw them once before, back at Boy Scout Camp
Manatoc, near Akron, where they were merely a natural
wonder. They emerged around our tents as we slept, and,
when we woke, the ground and the slender plantations
of trees were aflutter with living chrysoprase. Our scout-
master was not very helpful, being a bit phobic in the face of
it, batting his arms and screaming at the unmoved throngs.

The insects don't seem natural at all this time, but
rather, as though the preacher were actually onto something, wonders prodigious with rumor of time and destiny. Next time they come I will feel—what? Indifference?
Irritation? Wisdom? Perhaps I'll be once again reminded
of the poets, of the songs without weight, the lives without
shadow. Only in dreams will I dare to take the analogy
between artists and cicadas to its end, wondering why we
should be so blessed in their comings and their goings,
and yet so uncertain as to what to do with them, wondering what power summons them out of night just when they
are gorgeous and packed tight with venereal song.

67

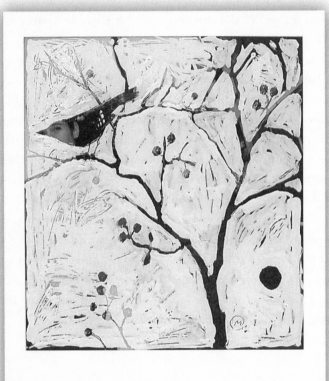

The Golden City

IN COLLEGE I SKIPPED CLASSES TO HIKE. I used to head
out when there was one hour of twilight left, or an hour
yet before the first twinkle of morning. Driving to church
or the market, I pull over to investigate a blossoming April
wood—I take what excuses come to set my feet on fern and
loam. But I have hiked—flat-out, just-for-the-sake-of-it
hiking—only twice this year. One of those times was today,
my birthday, the first of September. I am a Virgo, Libra
rising, moon in Taurus. I don't know what all that means,
but I repeat it for people who do.

I go hiking on my birthday, when I can. It gives me time

to think over the preceding year, over all the years that preceded it, to draw up some sort of account. One thing I cannot account for is this recent neglectfulness, nature-wise. Was the scraping of the cicadas in my own sweet-gum wilderness enough? In former days there was never anything important enough to postpone a hike. What does it say of me that things have changed so radically? Hiking was something I was good at, something with visible rewards (*Hey look, it's all right, I'm writing a* book), something that I gained a name for doing. It was something that, beyond all, I had loved. I feel like someone who mastered a complicated instrument in his youth and now never practices, never takes the thing out of its case except on rare occasions, when he touches the bow tentatively to the strings and hopes for the best.

Well, I'm still good at it, off the peak of my prime or not.

As I say, I nearly always hike on my birthday. It is purposeful activity to disguise the fact that, generally, nothing else is planned by anyone. It is also nearly always—and I claim no credit for this—a day of the most surpassing loveliness, sultry, golden brown, roofed with blue, the peaceful sleep of summer.

I pull my pickup off the Blue Ridge Parkway at Beaver Dam Gap onto an oblong of gray pavement. Beyond the edges of the pavement, between my truck and the deep woods, is a wilderness of gold and green, spun in small circles by the mountain breeze. My eyes choose an odd, low perspective suggested by the myriad of bumblebees thronging the flowers. From this perspective, the patch of late summer blossoms becomes a golden city, tall, branched, mobile, thronged at the top by the glitter and hurry of insects. The trees beyond are so huge and remote as to be irrelevant. The mountains are literally invisible. I have taken the eyes of a bee. The world is twenty feet wide and six deep. It is hot, clear, redolent, ablaze, the sky behind and above a luminous Dutch blue.

The main flower is *Helianthus annus,* the common sunflower. Partridge pea, mustard, goldenrod modulate the yellow of the sunflowers without departing from it. Here and there within the shimmer of gold appear accents of the magenta stems of pokeweed, the dusty pink of joe-pye, the silver pink of a kind of milkweed I have never seen before, erect, silky umbels like frost on pink bouquets. Most of the roadside is gold. Eleven fat bumblebees service one clump of sunflowers. There are at least fifty clumps of sunflowers. The dull hum when the breeze dies is the jewel-backed bees at their labor. Above them flutter small purplish butterflies, unnatural looking, like shreds of white cloth in black light. Above *them* flap enormous black swallowtails, casting shadows on the sunflower leaves far larger than the circling vultures cast on the oaks and the bare face of the mountain.

Under the stalks of the golden city the mountainside slopes down, though how far and how soon is difficult to tell under the vegetation. I ease in carefully, feeling the way with my shoes. As I go, I disturb grasshoppers and katydids, great green cows of the meadow, flopping enormously against my ankles, creatures grown fat with the bounty of summer. Amid the stalks lurk mantises, tigers of that land, grown in proportion and ferocity to feed on the available prey. You do not expect an insect to be so big, so sleek, so intimidating, with such jewel-like, expressionless hunter's eyes. B-grade monster movies violate nature in that an insect lacks lungs and, taking air through its skin and therefore requiring a very high surface-to-mass ratio, can never be big enough to menace a person, much less a city. Still, these cold-eyed mantises are big enough.

I skirt the edge of the field and enter deep forest. As the flowers of the light were golden, the flowers of the shade are blue and lavender. Some of the creatures of the light follow the regular paths into the shade of the trees. Asters spread themselves in blue frost at the path's edge. Grasshoppers ricochet through a meadow eight inches wide on the sides of the walk, where light leaks in and the herbs of the field endure for several hundred yards. Some of the milkweed has gone to seed, with paisley-shaped seedpods that look like perching green budgies. A patch of fungus had grown on one of the pods, and it is thronged by tiny red beetles, like minuscule cattle at a bloom of something sweet in a green meadow. There is nothing much to see at the wide angle, once you have registered the swaying trees against blue light. The show is small and close, where things are being riddled and blackened by the last hunger before frost.

Summer has been long, and everything is worse for the wear. A pink turtlehead was gnawed by something until it's but a shred of blossom waving at the end of a bare stalk. The blue-black berries of Solomon's seal hide under fronds sometimes all but eaten away. Why one Solomon's seal frond is a tattered ruin and the next is untouched I don't know. Nothing, apparently, eats the berries, which hang round, perfect, almost metallic in the blue shade.

The trees roundabout are smallish oaks. This was a bald, perhaps in living memory, growing up now into deep forest. The greatest trees, a few enormous mature oaks, a few towering tulips, are very old, many dying or dead, turned into silver columns riddled by woodpecker holes. They once stood nearly alone in great stony open spaces, like Graveyard Fields ten miles to the south, bare now, awaiting the return of its gradual camouflage of trees. At one point, the granite ribs of the mountain break through the soil. Nothing very big grows there, and the canopy parts into a vista of six ridges of the Appalachians, the farthest perhaps thirty miles away, fence after stone fence, north to south, graduating in color from deep green to smoky pale blue, like a painter's manual of how to depict distance.

Twenty-five feet away, on a tree trunk, a bat preens and combs, its wings folded at its haunches like the legs of a frog. It has been hunting in broad daylight over the boggy stream that divides us, returning to its tree to groom. It flutters within two feet of my face. Now and then I can hear its tiny chirpy noises. Amazingly, it is fishing, for it scrapes the black, still water with its claws, sometimes deeply, jerks its legs up. Suddenly there is a flash of silver, which I assume is a tiny fish it is throwing into its muzzle. I consider that it has not detected me, but even were it "blind as a bat," it would have heard me hauling my big body through the squirrel corn. I speak to it to make sure. It raises its neat red head, looks at me with a "yes, I know" expression, and goes back to chewing its food. Rhetorically I use "it" to refer to the creature, but that is a translation from the "he," which comes spontaneously to my tongue. "He" is a suave little man in the morning sun, a bit of a dandy, busy about the business of the forest, sated on the clean produce of the stream. I have blundered into his airy apartment, but he is a fine host, neither ignoring me wholly nor flapping indignantly away. In the hasty, acquisitive way of my kind I think I ought to remember this scene, catalog it, add the cinnamon-colored diurnal fishing bat to my internal life list and move on. Something stops me. I do not want to go. The second I recognize I do not want to go, I hear myself gasping. The bat has leaned back from his perch into the light, stretching, his little eyes squinted so only a row of diamonds leaks out under the lids, the outstretched wings translucent with the morning blaze, the fur flashing copper and mahogany and Crayola orange.

He is the most beautiful creature I have ever seen.

I try to work this fact into my conception of the world. It's not supposed to be a bat. It's not supposed to be today, me so unprepared for visions, six yards from the parkway. Beauty should have more fanfare.

Eventually one has to move on, even from this. As I walk, I am naming the names. I am not as good at that as I used to be, when I came to the forest with a backpack chock-full of twig keys and field guides. Two hours would pass and I would have penetrated ten feet into the woods, but I would by God know each frond and fungus. Many I still remember. Many I recognize by family resemblance. Many I have forgotten, and I think that's okay. I imagine that the flora might even be relieved not to be noticed, not this time to be part of the inevitably withering chronicles of men.

Reading the journals of Dorothy Wordsworth, one finds in her the same impulse to incantatory magic, the naming for the sake of naming, the sight of the thing to be cherished even if no conclusion or coherent visions follow: this quality of moonlight, that effect of mist on the low cliffs, none of it coming to a narrative point, but always for the sake of the things themselves, power in the mere enumeration of powers.

What I remember I say, rustily trying out the magic charm:

    sassafras
    hazel
    jewelweed
    turtlehead
    Turk's-cap lily
    cobra lily
    vireo
    hawk shape sailing, far away.
    female ovenbird . . . is that? Heavily streaked breast, too gray
    and blunt for an ovenbird, maybe. My eyes are failing.

It occurs to me finally why I am putting such stock in naming today. On the TV the other night was a special about the coming Great Extinction, like the Great Extinction that annihilated the dinosaurs, but this one caused by us, a single species wiping out a half million other species, the world our grandfathers knew never to be known again, sans rhino, sans elephant, sans walrus, sans what might have been an ovenbird. The time limit given in the program was a century and a half. A century and a half to wipe out the evolutionary labor of ten million years. I didn't believe it. I couldn't believe it. Mere hysteria, hyperbole to get a grant. And yet here I am, counting, naming, recording, as though someday men might have only my chronicle to remember by.

Recent informal reading, one of those don't-tell-the-kids-at-school books, had been David Drake's *Tyrannosaur*. Now, *Tyrannosaur* postulates a time machine developed by the Israeli military. Their preferred use for it is to change history, by, say, setting down a platoon of paratroopers in Jerusalem in 70 A.D. to prevent the destruction of the temple, but the thing can't be aimed very well, not at first, even within a hundred years of a target, so they content themselves with making big bucks by setting rich hunters down in the Cretaceous and letting them bang away at truly big game. A T. rex is brought forward to the twenty-first century for I forget what reason, and then, when it is returned to its native time, infects its whole world with the parrot fever (it's a proto-bird, remember) it has picked up in the future (the disease having developed after the death of the dinos, you see, and their having consequently no immunity). And *that's* what caused the extinction of the dinosaurs but left the piddling mammals intact. Okay, so it's a ripping yarn, but what it shows additionally is a sort of spreading and pervading species-wide guilt, the suspicion that human predations have been so voracious their effects reach even into the distant past.

We all claim to be bored by details in the old stories, yet what would we not give now for an item-by-item inventory of Priam's palace, say, just this many bronze vessels shaped like serpents, just this many lengths of brown linen, just this many pull toys for the play of tragic princes. What would I not give for the tally of the polar forests of Antarctica, while the world lay yet under the dome of carbon dioxide, warm even in the six-month winter dark, and salamanders the size of pickups lumbering through the polar ferns. What was lost in the past, though, need not be lost again. Not this time. No. That's why I became a writer. Nothing will be lost. I will write down everything—red oak, pin oak, hemlock, spicebush, gray squirrel—hoping that my lists remain the part that children skip in years to come, a finical bore rather than a sad necrology.

I can't explain why I am in love with minute particularity. Maybe just my bad eyes. Maybe my conviction that, though masses and categories remain, it is the particular that can be tragically lost.

I DON'T EXPECT ANYBODY to be in the forest today (it's *my* day), but I meet a family at the edge of the deep trees: young wife, young husband, a child on his father's shoulders. I look carefully at their faces: calm, blank, stupefied by the beauty of the morning, with the seraphic vacancy of Greek statuary. Perhaps they are not even fully conscious. Perhaps they are sleeping figures visible for a moment in their own phantasm, led into the forest by the guardians of dreams. I wave, and the wife waves back like one from some remote age, like one from the bottom of the sea.

I climb the steep slope, the steepest next to blue Pisgah himself. I have come up fast, like a fearless animal running through the undergrowth. I sit and listen now, breathing hard, trying to hear the forest over the sound of my gasping. A sound comes through the forest, a sound of running and laughing. I wait. At last a woman, the young mother I saw moments before, lunges into my clearing. She's running a path I struggled up bent almost double with effort. She is running and smiling, laughing sometimes in delight at her own speed. She is a black woman running in the green-gold forest. She is Artemis. She is the guardian. A few minutes later her son and husband trudge up the incline much as I did. I say to the boy, "Your mama's way ahead."

The sweating father answers, "She almost always is."

I wait for the tumult of their passing to settle. Though I'm never wholly out of earshot of the cars on the parkway, though the wind roars in the upper branches, the overall sensation is of quiet. The woods are full of sounds that are quieter than silence, the hush of the lifted branches, the peace of the bent-back tulip crowns. I hear a strange sound, always behind me, like the rhythmic placing of soft hooves on soft earth. I whirl to see what's there, and the movement is violent enough to reveal that the sound is water sloshing in the bottle in my pack. The deer are asleep in their dappled glades, the raccoons in the cool hollows of their trees. The insects and I are all that's abroad at this hour. Morning, evening, night are full of turbulent life. Go in the afternoon if you wish to hear yourself in the forest, your own thoughts coming to meet you after circling the world. Whales can hang suspended in the planet-girdling Antarctic Ocean and blast out sonar that will come back to them after circling the world. At the top of the hill, I feel like that, my thoughts soaring and returning after compassing all the world I am likely to know.

Amid all this quiet, I realize that these thoughts have been harsh and turbulent. Birthdays are hard; comparisons between what you thought would be and what has arrived unbidden. You think of the time you've spent, and what you have to show for it. You think of what your parents expected when they went through the labor of you, what they might have been thinking (if they were thinking at all) on the night of your conception, which, in my case, could well have been New Year's Eve, everybody expecting something new and wonderful at the midpoint of a century. You add up whom you've loved and who has loved you, and suspect that the lists are grossly uneven. The call of a bird or the sharp slap of a branch may bring you out of it, but the somber suggestions are planted.

I realize I went to the forest on my birthday not merely

because of the perfection of the weather. I went because my present life is caught on a wheel of hours, and the forest is timeless. I am dying in a far country and do not know the way back home, while the forest finds its own youth every year. To enter the wild at any time is to enter the wild for the first time. You are a child still, again and always, and this is the forest you wandered into then with wonder and delight. All wilderness at all times is part of a single place and a single moment, outside the chronologies of men. Though this walk is six hundred miles and forty years from my first walk in the forest, neither the space nor the time matter. It is the same place, the same moment, and in them I am the same child, the same infinite potential. It is another country, and I am another creature in it, one I recognize more clearly than the man I am in the measured valley and the city beyond. Is this retrogression, restoration, a trick of memory, or a fact? Does the forest really keep one time and man another, or is it I who keep two times, one for the city of men, one for the golden city of the mountain, dividing my life between them, unable to assemble the full courage to choose one and deny the other? The cicadas have one day that is seventeen years. Ephemerida have a lifetime that is a single hour.

No need to decide, not today. Let fear and frustration settle into the pale green mosses, let them cool there, be sucked up into the million roots and be sublimed into the air. I will go home and not answer the phone for the rest of the night. I will allow myself to think that all the unanswered calls are wishing me well. The cicadas are almost silent.

I SIT ON A LOG on the south bank of Bent Creek. I sat down so I could write a poem that came into my head. That was three hours ago. I am still writing. The shadows of trees have moved across the page. The light has changed from red gold to wheat. A pair of cardinals have come and gone in the osiers, again and again, forgetting after the first half hour that I am not a natural thing. Dace dart in the shallows, and a spider spins from the corner of my book back to a corner of a river rock. It is a green spider. Jade over malachite. I will tell people this and they will not believe it. I tell the spider my poem.

Where this gush, this white rush comes from at my age I do not ask. It was not like this, even at the first, when I had to creep into my room at night, secret and alone, to meet the words coming out of me like shamed lovers, tentative, one, two at a time, waiting their turn.

Now I sit with my knees pointing out of the brush, widespread and shameless, scribbling so fast the words come out crumpled. Hours afterward I will spend under my study lamp, smoothing them out, beating them into gold and silver. Hikers and cyclists pass saying, "You must be a poet," with that expression people get. Now I don't even bother to deny, don't even try to cover the page with my arm, pretending I was doing nothing.

And I think of my friends who are dead and who died

in futility and despair. I think of the ghosts moving from bed to work and bed again, and I call their names to them, and they call mine back to me, but they are not comforted. And I know in all the corners of the world the mutilated cry out, holding the tatters of their bodies, and the eyes of children glaze with hunger, and human mouths are turned into muzzles, howling, and the pale skirts flutter from the rooftops, heading down—while I sit under twenty sweet trees writing my little poems, while I have found mercy deeper than all waters.

I cannot explain this.

In a moment I will finish my poem, will set my boot heels in the emerald dazzle, and go on.

The Well of Memory

I AM A PLATONIST because I know things I have no reason to know and had no occasion to learn. I am a Platonist because a long time ago I read a story the Cambridge neo-Platonists came up with. It seems that every soul at death is given the choice of whether to drink from Lethe, the river of forgetfulness, or from the well of memory. Nearly all drink from Lethe, of course, but a few, the teachers and prophets of the coming world, sacrifice peace and drink from the well of memory. When I asked myself which I had drunk from, it seemed that I too had taken a good swig of forgetfulness, but, somehow, before I was through drinking, I had changed my mind, run to the well of memory, and drank of that, too, whereby my memory of ancient things is fragmentary and indistinct, but haunting and ineradicable. I tell people I remember the slant of light through forests that are now the bottom of the sea. I tell them I remember the bird song of the Mesozoic. They think I am joking.

FOR YEARS I HAVE PLAYED THE GAME of trying to remember the earliest possible personal experience. I am able to go very far back, though the experiences thus fished from the subconscious are invariably solitary or so apparently trivial that no one else is likely to remember them. They are, therefore, unverifiable. Those I mention to my father, he either does not remember or remembers very differently. But there's one from very long ago indeed that I haven't mentioned to my father, because I know he wasn't in it:

I am walking a path down the center of a bright field. The field lies between a forest and a lake. I am very small, and the grasses wave over my head on either side. I am following somebody. The somebody I am following is a good way ahead and may not know I am following him. I am desperate to catch up, though not desperate enough to cry out to him. I feel he is at once available and forbidden — like a god, one with more sophistication might have said.

He enters the dim forest and disappears. After a moment's hesitation, I enter, too. He has stopped. He is waiting for me. He is very tall, slender for a grown man, and turned so that his facial features, though partially visible and sharp, are indistinct. He wears a hat with wide brim, a fishing hat. There are hooks and tied flies in the ribbon of the hat. He wears a gray coat. Now, the question is, who is he? He is a male I love and fear at once. I do not think he's my father, because my father never knew what the man is about to tell me. I believe he is my grandfather, my father's father, Oliver. If so, it is one of the few moments of real contact we had in our lives. He was a secretive man, and even his sons, my father and uncle, didn't know him well. Perhaps he is somebody I made up, but if so, my imagination that day was a flame of etching fire, for all is clear, bright, unexpected, full of images, such as the tied flies, which I would not be able to identify for years later.

His posture tells me that I am welcome, but that I must not do anything too forward, must not ask questions or try to take his hand. I follow several steps behind through the cool forest. I am asking questions in my mind. He must hear, for he points here and there and begins to speak.

"Maple. There are two kinds. That's sugar maple. The other kind—over there—is red. Red maple. You can tell because high up, the red maple's branches turn a different color."

I freeze it desperately into my mind: *the red maple's branches turn a different color.*

"That there's the mayapple. See under the umbrella thing? The little white flower?"

Mayapple.

"Oak. Red oak. Points on the leaves. Think of needles, knives, the red of blood after they cut you. Red oak."

Red oak.

"That there. Indian turnip. What does it look like?"

I'm stupefied. I have no idea what it looks like.

"It looks like a preacher in a pulpit. That's its name, its other name. Jack-in-the-pulpit. Are you remembering this?"

I nod. *Jack-in-the-pulpit.*

"Basswood . . . tulip . . . white oak, see the rounded leaf ends . . . elm, two kinds, feel the back of the leaves.

Basswood . . . tulip . . . white oak . . . elm, two kinds . . . slippery, American . . .

Whoever the man is—and the more I think of it, the more I hope he was my grandfather—I recognize the vital importance, the sacred significance of what he is telling me. I hang onto every word. I set all the dials to "Remember." Furthermore, something inside me was mapping my own future course. It recognized even in that hour what I was meant to do. That must be why I held on so tightly to the moment, remembered so furiously. I was meant to lead people through the forest, pointing things out, telling their names, hoping that my pupils would fathom the absolute importance of purely *knowing*. Not that it would always be a forest, but it would be dark and secret, and I would take such delight in uttering the names—*Keats, Shakespeare, Gilgamesh*—that my hearers' own delight must be automatic.

He points to the trees and the herbs, and utters. I follow, trying to catch everything. The memory ends there. Perhaps all he needed to do was name one thing, so that, in a flash of revelation hard as the blow of a fist, I would know that all things *had* names, that all things were *beings* that could hide or reveal their secrets at the speaking of a word.

He gave me magic. I have been repeating this walk in the woods ever since. I have become a teacher. I knew how to teach long before I stepped into a classroom.

But one time only I tried to do it exactly as that mysterious man had done. I felt it was my duty, that something important had to be passed on *exactly*. Things are as they are, and at some point they are independent of our ideas about them.

I took my sister to the beech woods near my house and named the trees and the flowers for her. Still following in my grandfather's footsteps, I was neither very patient nor all that welcoming—I assumed that was part of the lesson—but I was precise, true. I have never asked my sister if she remembers that time. Someday I will.

I live very far from where I grew up, in the mountains, away from the rolling meadows and deep creeks of my home. But some of the spirits are here, the ones whose names I learned long ago. I can call to them and they answer. I am a Platonist because when I call one name, one spirit answers, and the name and the spirit are always one. For this reason, I am good at detecting frauds, even when the source of the fraudulence cannot always be identified. My hatred is far cannier—if less in all other aspects—than my love. I suspect this is generally true of people who believe the witness of the invisible.

I MEET LYNETTE FOR A WALK in the woods. Lynette is high priestess of a coven that meets in south Asheville. I have helped her and a couple of other Wiccan organizations from time to time, not really because I understand what they are up to, but because we seem to have the same enemies. Once I asked Lynette how she became a high priestess, and it turns out one can give oneself the honor. I think that is a wonderful convenience.

Lynette hears that I am a nature writer. For some reason this makes her angry. She makes that face people make when they have heard something too absurd to credit. I ask her why this makes her angry, and she says I have no right to interpret the natural world until I have seen it through her eyes (she says "the goddess's eyes," but I interpret). People like me look at nature only from the outside, she maintains, while she can enter into the heart of things. I try to fathom what exactly she means, to understand how she might look at things differently than I. I tell her I'm stumped. I ask her what, exactly, *is* the "heart of things," and she smiles that smile that tells you that you'll never learn.

"You're an academic," she says. "There'll be no getting through." But finally she agrees to teach me. She agrees to take me into the forest to teach me the wisdom of the grandmothers. She admonishes me to try the "natural way," to come into the forest with her and meet the virtuous plants and keep silent and learn. Keeping silent is very important. She asks me three times if I am willing to do this. I am. I am actually very good at keeping silent. I am the opposite of a chatterbox. Only on the third asking does it occur to me to retort, "Are *you* willing?" But she is the teacher. I will keep silent and learn.

We start at an entry of the Shut-In, off the Blue Ridge Parkway. I want to ask her what we're looking for, but I remember her admonition to silence, so I wait until she says, "Know what we're looking for?"

"No."

"Ginseng."

Fine, good, we're looking for ginseng. After half an hour of walking, she kneels down on the forest floor, her hands around a middle-sized, oddly shaped plant.

"Ginseng," she says, and begins to tell me the virtue of the plant. Virility, energy, circulation, the immune system. I nod at the useful information and keep to myself the fact that the plant she is kneeling by is jack-in-the-pulpit and not ginseng at all. She says a prayer and pulls the jack-in-the-pulpit up by the roots.

"The prayer is vital," Lynette says, "to keep from imbalancing the forest. I would forbid most people to pick this plant. You must show respect. No harvest without thanks. Now, what is this?"

"You called it ginseng."

I'm thinking: *jack-in-the-pulpit. Under the purple-striped tent, under the folded spathe, the spadix sits like a weapon in a costly sheath. Called Indian turnip, its corm can save the starving. The gorgeous parts are not the flower.*

"See this?" she croons. "The blue, the little blue ones? They should be easy to remember because they are forget-me-nots."

She says "forget-me-nots" loudly and slowly, as though I were retarded, or a foreigner.

The blue is, in fact, speedwell, the herbalist's veronica. Not entirely blue, blue white, of a cloudy heaven or a pale pure turquoise. Close up, the blossoms are seen to radiate a blueness outward from the heart. If any of the legends of the flowers is happy, I have not heard it. Speedwell, Veronica's flower, bears the imprint of a face, a beard, a crown or corona smeared by sweat or blood. At a distance, the sky-blue of the flower tricks the eye to whiteness. Because the flowers bear that image, they are said to heal: *veronica cleanseth the blood of all corruption.* Whether or not, it cures the wasted places. It can take a whole field.

Lynette has plucked a handful of veronica. She is scolding me for not paying attention. "You're off in an intellectual reverie while the mockingbirds are singing their hearts out for you!"

I need not observe there are on the mountain no mockingbirds. A lone thrush revs up in the underbrush, subsides, lets fly with an ambush of round tones, like half-liquid pearls. Lynette smirks at me in triumph. Let's see who now knows nature. Still, she's led me to the place where the thrush throbs in a red thicket, and if she thinks it's mockingbirds, it's just as beautiful.

"You must start over. You must go at it from the inside. You must have a *sense* of the wild world. You must *listen*. Now, the vervain—"

I look around for what she might be calling vervain. Ah!—the rattlesnake plantain. I steel myself against her pulling of it, but she does pull it, the only one we have seen in the forest.

"Why did you pull that, Lynette? It was—"

"It offered itself to us. If you would just listen, you would understand."

I start easing us toward the forest edge, where the light of the bald meets the shade of the forest. There's poison ivy there. I want her to listen, pluck it, lecture on it. I want to hear what she'll call it. I want to see what she'll spread on the itch, and what she'll say to explain how the red vines lied with their subtle voices. She will never be able to claim I didn't keep silent, just as she ordered. She sails past the poison-ivy patch. The goddess has saved her.

Lynette pulls herself up a slope by the limb of a hickory. She says "hickory," and I cry out with her triumph. She smiles at me, radiantly, smiles upon one who, at last, is beginning to get it.

"Well, what did you think?"

She's asking, so I make bold to reply. "Lynette, you don't even know the names—"

"Details," she laughs with a toss of her shoulder. "Some of us are more concerned with power."

I consider what would have happened to Moses if, upon Sinai, he had called on Baal.

Back at the car, Lynette asks me what I have learned today. I say, "Plenty."

"Not what you expected, right?"

"No, Lynette, nothing like what I expected, at all."

I SIT IN THE SHADE planning a book of the plants, putting in their properties and virtues. I'm half asleep, so their beautiful names hover between the waking world and the world of dreams. I call them, at first randomly, but then properly, and when they hear their proper appellations, they answer.

I am a Platonist because I have heard things answer to their proper names.

ANGELICA: by the sea, by running water, tall, celery-like in the stalk, celery-like to taste, but better. Flowers like a tattered cloud, like a round hill shot with snow. Good for digestion, a body cleanser.

BALM OF GILEAD: flat leaves shaking in the least wind, crowded together in the meadow light, before the forest giants come. The giants of the open places, away to the west, where they shake like rigged masts under the thunderheads.

CHICKWEED: white flowers like the stars children draw. The least of all herbs, left alone, can take over a field, a county. Survives any freeze, blooms while snow still lies on its leaves. Can save the starving.

DOGWOOD: the ancient one, older then the hills it grows upon, pushed aside by the dragons of the prime. Snow after the snow in the depths of the forest.

ELDERBERRY: purple stain on the mouth, the shirt, of one hungry for the bittersweet drupes, the taste of sweet and smoke and water and purple. The Indians hollowed the twigs, blew through them for flutes, "the tree of music." Vitamins packed close as purple in an amethyst.

FERN: even the dogwoods call this one "grandmother." The old ones thought its seeds, being invisible, granted invisibility. Out of the wet rock, out of the waste places, it could restore a world, if this world passed away.

GREAT MULLEIN: shooting like a rocket from a rosette of green fire. Taller than a man, it seeks the waste place, makes abundance out of ruin. Edible, like the whale, if anybody dares.

HICKORY: the autumn shimmerer, bronze gold, the treasure of the squirrels. My grandfather had a triple-trunked pignut that was the tallest tree in the world.

INDIAN: paintbrush, corn, rice, turnip, ginger, fig, lettuce, hemp: also the Indian pipe, the ghost plant, a saprophyte, like an herb taken from a cave, or from a distant planet where light adds no color.

JERUSALEM ARTICHOKE: not, of course, an artichoke, but a sunflower, ten feet tall, with the tiny flowers of a yellow daisy. Not from Jerusalem, either, but a native North American, used by the ancient ones for difficulties of the throat and lungs.

KELP: the sea wrack, the redwood of the deep, in swaying forests a hundred feet tall, the great-grandmother of the algae, the safety of the otters, the hunting grounds of the abalones in their tanks of pearl.

LILAC: by Grandmother's back porch, climbable by the child one was, the hanging grape shapes of white and lavender and—yes—of lilac, the spring perfume that haunts all springs to come.

MINT: square stems, opposing leaves, that scent so dear to us, so hateful to the slugs and leaf borers. Like most strong, heroic things, it must be bruised a little to yield its best.

NETTLE: some sting and some do not. Only thrusting your hand amid them will tell. Those that sting do so with the same poison as the bees and ants.

OAK: Odin's tree, and Zeus's, the tree of the Thunderers. Whispered god's words in Dodona long ago. The red oak holds its leaves through winter, sometimes the only color in a world of gray and white.

POKE: sweet in spring, bitter in the fall, sweet in the new sprouts, poison in the old growth. Its red berries make birds drunk when they eat them.

QUEEN ANNE'S LACE: the wild carrot, dusted with the summer of Midwestern roads, the flowers, yes, like lace, enduring in the vase, in the child's hand, one purple petal like one drop of blood, for remembrance.

ROSE: they are all roses, the cherries, the plums, the steeplebushes, strawberries, blackberries, apple, and, of course, the rose itself, red, white, golden, compass, mystic.

SASSAFRAS: it was the smell of sassafras which told Columbus's men not to despair, land was near. Each tree has three different leaves, a mitten, a trefoil, and a spearhead, each root brims with aromatic fume.

TULIP: the tree, I mean, the magnolia's launch toward heaven, clean boled, the sky spearer, the ancient one, marching south with the glaciers, north with the coming of the ten-thousand-year delayed spring.

UMBRELLA PLANT: the mayapple, with its pale flower hidden, the green fruit, bitter, edible, hidden deeper, green within green.

VIOLET: five petaled, white, purple, blue, yellow, striped, near black, nodding modestly under the blare of the trilliums, the white tremor of the bloodroots. The tombs of saints, opened, exude an odor of violet.

WATER LILY: like an animal, sleeping by night, waking by day, fragrant: a pure beauty rising from black mud, therefore a symbol of the mysteries of the human soul.

XANTHIUM: the cocklebur, like some men, loving at first sight, clinging forever after.

YARROW: the woundwort, the soldier's friend, they stem the flow of blood.

ZINNIA: the summer flower, the going-back-to-school flower, the only annual I will suffer in my garden, pink, red, scarlet, pumpkin, white, almost black, almost green, the flower on which the seasons change.

OH, I HEAR THE VOICE OF A CHILD in the garden of dreams say, *Let us start again . . . let's do it over! Anemone, bloodroot, cattail, dodder . . .*

Tokens

I START UP THE PATH from the Big Ridge overlook. I think there's a message in the fact that the path entrance is overgrown with brambles, and one tears through, if at all, with little grazes and nicks on one's ankles. I think it might be a warning to some and an invitation to others—an invitation to me, for instance. Quests begin this way—am I really in the mood? It almost makes me turn and go another way. Six feet in, though, thicket yields to deep forest, high, dark woods snaking up toward the slopes of Mount Pisgah. The biota changes sharp as a whip crack from meadow to woodland, except along the path where a measure more light allows the goldenrod and asters to straggle a good way into the shadows. When I stop for a moment, I realize that around me reigns the most miraculous silence. No wind. No bird—though the silent shadow of a vulture crosses and recrosses, more silent seeming than nothing at all. I have been climbing pretty fast, and in that silence what I hear best is the sound of my pulse in my ears. This is disturbing. I take my pulse to see if something is wrong. I begin up the trail again, comforting myself with the din of my own passage.

I archaeologize as I walk. This hill has not been forest forever. The oaks and tulips are small, slender, probably not much older than I, though, of course, much taller. Many of the true giants are dead or dying. The remnants of their peers endure as great white columns visible upright in the gloom of the trees, banquet tables for the woodpeckers; some of the dead trees are quite overthrown, their long, greened-over bodies disappearing in the undergrowth, clear pools and fern gardens in the pit from which their roots lift into the air.

The quiet is thoroughly blasted when a grouse explodes from the undergrowth nearly at my feet. The point of all that squawking and flapping is to startle and disorient a predator, and it certainly has that effect on me. I pause a moment while my heart settles back from panic rhythm. A blue jay takes up the grouse's cause and commences screaming at me from the treetops. The jay takes me on as its personal harassment project, dogging, or rather birding, me at every turn of the trail. I wonder if there is something to be accomplished by this, or if the jay, has, as I have, simply decided to pursue some impractical project to its end. I am, after all, climbing this mountain to no other purpose than the doing. What profit the jay should get out of following me is hard to imagine, unless I begin chopping a tree, unless I build a campfire and begin to cook, unless I should collapse and die on the trail. Maybe it is not scolding me. Maybe it is warning me. Is there something ahead, in the undergrowth, that he can penetrate and I cannot, lurking, of which I should be wary? My conviction that all days are the same in the forest opens the door—an imagined one, anyway—onto the lumbering horrors of the Pleistocene. I keep my eyes and ears open, giving the jay the benefit of the doubt.

On the top of a ridge, the canopy opens suddenly. Here are oaks, spearing toward the sky with adolescent vigor, but mostly the trees are locusts, the greatest black locusts I have ever seen, thick, tall, remarkably straight, though the crowded conditions of the forest improve the posture of all trees. This place must be miraculous in the spring, with a tossing roof of white perfume. I have stood on this spot maybe fifty times; it amazes me that I have never noticed the locusts before. I've been looking forward and down, sometimes at the Turk's-cap lilies, sometimes at the trail, where I know there to be copperheads. The dark V of the vulture passes over, circles, passes over again. It is certain that he can see me through the gaps, though whether I am what he watches I don't know. The ancient Irish left their dead on the mountainsides for the wild beasts to pick and clean, and then buried or burned the bones. Perhaps the vulture smells my Celtic blood. Perhaps he is merely waiting, for me, for anything to reach the door of this life and pass through, leaving a mound of protein behind. I would certainly cooperate, when the time comes, if I could find a way around the authorities who make the dead their business. I wonder if the human bodies that are found sometimes in the forest have been picked over by vultures. The news reports have never mentioned that occurrence. Maybe the vultures make exceptions for human bodies, passing them by with holy dread. Somehow I think not.

The unusual bounty of light under the locusts allows the forest floor to bloom. The word "bloom" is symbolic and general in this case: the major stands are enormous ostrich plume ferns—which, of course, do not bloom at all. Some of them come to my shoulders. Some, farther off, shake with mysterious bodies—perhaps the breeze's, perhaps not—passing through them. They are rich, dark, Mesozoic. Once I alight on the word "Mesozoic," my imagination seizes the image and runs. *What is really causing the ferns to tremble on a windless day? What was the blue jay really squawking at? What is really squawking under the skin of the blue jay?* I expect deep hissing from the deep shade. I expect a bird with claws and teeth to blast from the thickets, rasping and cawing, startling me as the grouse already has done. Why I think the bird songs of the Mesozoic would be harsh I don't know. Why shouldn't hesperornis have the haunting music of the loon, whose shape and habits it prefigured? Why shouldn't the bird songs of the Mesozoic—such as there were—have been beautiful? And, as the Mesozoic was a *very* long time, why should they not have been as various and abundant as any human imagination can take in? For that matter, why wouldn't the dinosaurs, out of which the birds were even then springing, have themselves been musical? Would birds simply have made song up out of nothing, or could it too have been an inheritance from the knife-toothed carnosaurs that seem to have been their forefathers? Nothing is too unlikely. Reptiles rose from the amphibia, who—frogs and toads and Lord knows what else once upon a time—warbled with the first voices of the earth.

I allow my mind to wander this path for a while. The jay, still rattling in the trees, offers a template for the bird-songs of the Mesozoic, which I fill in as I walk: here the warbling carnosaurs, there the bellbird duckbills . . . still there the mocking diplodocus. I am filled, as I always am at such times, with the most unutterable longing. I want to hear those lost creatures. I want to believe that the songs I make up for them now are not *just* made up, but channeled somehow out of the deep past. In J.R.R. Tolkien's *Silmarillion* someone mentions that Valinor, the earthly paradise, is a place where all the creatures that ever were on Middle Earth are still alive. This to me is paradise indeed. Given sight of a living brachiosaur, of one of those giant salamanders of the dawn, of a beaver the size of a rowboat, of Megalodon heaving the waves over its terrible back, I think I would shut my mouth in contentment, like Arjuna before the revealed Krishna.

ON SOME CAMPUS FOR A CONFERENCE that was rather vaguely concerned with religious themes in poetry, I was asked what my conception of the earthly paradise was. I don't know what I actually said, but later, addressing the question in peace on the pages of my journal, I wrote, "Ireland with dinosaurs."

A GRAY CLOUD RISES, catches for a moment on a high peak, slides on toward the northwest. This cloud is an extended, tenuous streamer of the hurricane chugging its way up the Atlantic coast, putting summer to an end from Hatteras to the mouth of Chesapeake Bay. Before the Great Ice melted, Chesapeake Bay was the last hundred miles of the Susquehanna River. In an age before this one, my narrow green valley was a Himalayan cleft, snowbound, howling with blizzards. Mount Mitchell away to the east and Pisgah a mile to the south comprised the roof of the world before this world. Before the continents scurried apart, I could walk from here to Africa. I could clamber down the Atlas or the Pyrenees and be in my own backyard. Amid the rocks the birds, some unimaginable feathered sparks recognizable as sparrows, odd as creatures of the moon, were singing.

Down in the city, the ground on which the foundations of my little house rests has been uplifted into mountains for a quarter billion years. Forgotten mothers of the world drank from the rock-studded falls. Tyrannosaurs prowled the plains stretching away toward the inland sea to the west. A heartbeat ago, mammoths, camels, horses, wolverines, saber tooths, man-sized rodents, buffalo the size of elephants, lions the size of compact cars, hyena-like monstrosities bigger than bears, condors with wingspreads to blot out the sun, beside which my circling vulture is a toy, gleaned the bounty of the clefts and valleys.

To name these things, to think of them, fills me with dissatisfaction. Even before I knew for sure of their existence I longed for these creatures, for anything that was *not here* and *not now*. Discovering that they had demonstrably been was merely confirmation. Actual fossils were the ghosts of a conviction already laid down in the heart. Memory is longer than any of us is willing to admit. Though I cannot say I miss these creatures directly, I miss *something,* something that was created, prospered, and then was lost, but which was, unfathomably, my kin.

I am *lonely*. The reason why I am a naturalist is that I am lonely. The reason why I am a poet is that I am lonely. The reason why I am—well, I don't even know what to call it—a religious fanatic, maybe—is that I am lonely. Among my most secure proofs for the existence of God is that someone must have taken delight in the creatures that lived before any of us were here to take delight. Hating as I do to sound like Bishop Berkeley, it is still a truth that someone must have laughed at the gawky dinosaur babies, gaped at the wingspreads of the pterosaurs, cradled the shivering mothers of the orchids, or there would have been no point to it. What a waste of exuberance if no one had been watching all the while! Just as there is no beauty without sacrifice, there is no beauty without observation. I am a faithful evolutionist, but I do not believe for a moment that evolution is propelled, ultimately, by anything other than soul, and the soul, in this world, by longing. This will bring hatred on me from both sides, from the people of the Book and the people of the Microscope, but I know what I know.

What brings me out of the reverie is a glimpse of another color, a discord in the green, a red-gold flash startling in all that primeval shadow. It is a copperhead snake. I expected it, but I didn't *expect* it. "It" is two copperhead snakes, fifteen feet from each other and the closest about the same distance from me, taking advantage of the broken canopy for a dose of afternoon sun. The sight is exhilarating. I hear from me that intake of breath that comes from beholding a wonder, a breathless gasp, covered quickly lest it ruin the moment. I know from past experience that the snakes will allow me to get quite close and that the odds against their attacking without severe provocation are almost infinite. I mean to provide no provocation. As I approach the nearer one, I realize that I have been fully shaken from my fantasy about the bird songs of the Mesozoic, and the reason is that the snakes seem so *modern*. There is nothing Jurassic, nothing dinosaurian about them, nothing outlandish or exotic. They are sleek, compact, familiar, even to some degree technological, as though designed by engineers as much as by natural forces. It's not that I see that many copperheads to have grown blasé, but that their affect, the shape they take in space, is plausible and contemporary. They look *right*. I imagine that is how we will know aliens if and when they visit, even if they imitate shapes known to us; something will just look *wrong*.

The nearer snake, now situated almost between the toes of my shoes, is beautiful. It has arrayed itself as if to best advantage, in full sun, so the red-copper-gold, umber-striped expanse of its body looks like a sinuous, dropped jewel, set against a complementary background of green. It has felt me through the dirt and begins to move ahead reluctantly, keeping to the path. Though I have already said that I do not expect aggression from the snakes, their keeping to the path disturbs me. What if I can't get around? What if I have to turn back? I won't try to leap over them, for rule one of snake association is "Don't do anything startling," and that would be startling. Finally, the snake veers to one side. I give him plenty of time to find safety in the ferns before I move to the spot where he had been. I bend down and touch the ground that the copperhead's body had just vacated. I don't know what I expected, certainly not warmth. Maybe a spark of electricity, a token to take with me up the path.

When I stand up, I see that the other snake has wandered off, too. Though I have the path to myself now, any illusion that I had been "alone" is well shattered. The grouse, the vulture, the jay, the copperheads had their days changed by my pushing past the brambles onto their mountain. Through the ferns poke up tall stalks of Turk's-cap lilies, dusty pink clouds of joe-pye, frilly stands of jewelweed. Not here the orange of sunlit places, but yellow, the purest, pale, cool yellow in the world. Everywhere in the underbrush there are subtle twitchings and tremblings. I know the bodies of the copperheads, still warm from their sunbath, are pushing past the stalks of the jewelweed, darkening and dampening in the fern gloom. Mesozoic voices return. The shadow sweeping the treetops is way too large for a vulture's. Why anyone ever leaves the beaten path I can't imagine.

There is an evident quota on adventures for any given day, and I figure I've reached mine. Just as the urge to turn around, go home, catch up on schoolwork begins to strengthen, I see something caught in the jewelweed. It is a feather, but not merely a feather: the great wing primary of a hawk, as long as my arm from elbow to the finger joint past the knuckle, variegated through a harmony of browns. It is striped and spotted at once, tigerish. It is also perfect; it has been lying there at most since morning. Around it are tiny clumps of down from the same bird. Perhaps it caught something that put up a fight. Perhaps it was merely preening in the gray limbs above my head. When I pick the feather up, when I determine it is meant for me and that I will carry it home, I know I have to leave something behind in the forest of equivalent value. God knows what that will be.

I lift the feather into the light, turn it around. If asked what color its owner is, I would say "brown, with red on its tail," but certainly this bird is not "brown," or, if so, twenty

browns, from reddish buff to profound umber, paling at
the feather tips again to blond. This much subtlety, this
much labor to produce the single impression, *brown*. The
object is not "light as a feather," but pushes on my hand
with real weight. It exerts surprising lift when it catches a
breeze. *This is how it flies,* I think, *even a bit of wind on this feather
would lift.* I almost think it could lift me.

I'm still marveling at the gift from the forest floor when
my eyes focus a yard or two beyond the tip of the feather.
Here a tree has fallen and a glade has been opened, about
the dimensions of a king-sized bedspread. I've been standing still long enough contemplating the hawk primary—or
moving no more than could be explained by the freshen-
ing breeze—that the creatures of the glade have returned
to their daily business. The open space boils with juncos.
Black forest butterflies probe the tufts of joe-pye with
their long siphons. Something else . . . I work my bad
eyes into something resembling acuity, and see at the
base of the upturned tree the tiny body of a vole, rushing out from hiding, nibbling a stalk of grass or the stem
of a flower in two, rushing back to its lair with its fresh
green prize. The vole is very dark brown. When it runs
into a patch of sun, the light does not light up the fur,
as it often does with animals, but gets absorbed, so the
creature seems darker in the light than it does in the
shade. It has elected to spend exactly the same amount of
time in the open each time. Sometimes it can get the stalk
down in that time. Sometimes it scurries back to its hole
empty handed, as it were, and has to use the next sally to

complete the task. I believe that it waited for the juncos to become active, for the sound it makes in the grass is so like the sound they make that it would pass unnoticed amid their greater numbers and visibility.

The vole, the twittering juncos, the dappled sunlight moved a little this way and that by the breeze, mesmerize me. I stand there the better part of twenty minutes. The hawk feather is a real weight in my hand. I let my arm fall, slowly, so as not to disturb the show. Perhaps I broke the spell, or perhaps the vole had enough in its larder for the moment, but it is gone, and I can see juncos anytime, so I move on. There is still the question of what to leave behind in thanks for the tigerish feather. In my backpack is a bottle of water and a few pens. I wore no jewelry. Semen is often a correct offering, and one readily available, but I am not in the mood. When I reach the farthest point I intend to, it occurs to me to sing. So there I am on the last shoulder of stone before Pisgah, singing the bass line of a Russian church piece we're doing in church choir. I have changed the key so that it is low, as low as I can go, and I can go pretty low. My eyeballs tickle with the vibration. Yes. This was right, the right choice. It is the key the trees sing in as they rock on their roots in the wind. They have it sung to me, and I sing it back. Whatever its other effects, the song drives the nuisance jay from the treetops, the shadowing vulture from the air.

I AM NOT PARTICULARLY A PACK RAT. But I do keep a few tokens that I believe have been given to me by the world toward some end, spiritual or material.

The great hawk primary is stuck into a picture frame. From time to time it flutters to the ground of its own will.

Against the front-porch wall leans a stick, so sensuously twisted and so wound with bittersweet that it looks like a wizard's staff. It has leaned there for two years without apparent change.

In a box somewhere, the jawbone of an opossum, a bit of petrified wood, the clay marbles my father played with as a boy.

On the bottom of a shelf that otherwise holds CDs lie two smooth rocks lifted from the Tralee Bay, two gray oceanic sedimentaries, one divided down the center with a deposit of, I imagine, lava, from some unimaginable calamity of the elder days.

An emerald lies in a chest on my bookshelf, unmounted, clear, though not *quite* clear, like grass seen through shallow water or a film of rime.

Pale clay spheres sit in a glass jar on a shelf, where I can see them when I move from room to room. Earth colored, smooth as stones worked by the sea or a great river, they look natural, but they are not. They are the marbles my father played with when he was a boy in Maple Glen beside the Monongahela, in a world as finally, if not quite so anciently, past as that of the saber tooths.

In a blue glass container shaped like a swan, which I got at a yard sale for this exact purpose, rests a fossil of two trilobites. The fossil is artificially polished, naturally ink black, and displays the animals as if they were crawling over each other in some moment of horseplay half a billion years remote. There are times when I consider this my most precious possession, though it was bought for ten bucks from a rock shop in Charleston. For years it rested on the top of my computer screen, as a sort of muse, but it kept falling off and getting lost in papers and desk detritus, so I moved it to the swan box, where it is on my mind often enough to serve the same purpose.

These objects are precious to me for reasons that I cannot explain rationally. In this they are identical to most other holy objects, which are holy just because they are, and not because their holiness can be justified to the rational mind. Actual physical possession of these objects is not necessary. There were other holy objects in the past that I, when the moment called for it, gave away with a light heart. The fossil of raindrops in ancient mud. The god's eye woven for me at Ghost Ranch by my high school girlfriend. The almost-ruby ore plucked from the highest pool of the Pigeon River. The onyx and gold ring found in a pool at Roosevelt Ditch when I was thirteen, which I imagined was a token of a primeval king, fleeing before glaciers or enemies long ago. All of these are gone, given away, passed on to the next finder, but, as you see, no less present to my imagination. The next time I see her, I will give the hawk feather to my friend Ellen, who collects bird feathers. The best she had before this was from a swan on the Corrib, the river of Galway, but my Blue Ridge hawk easily trumps that. I know giving it away is the way to retain it in my heart.

"What thou lovest well remains; / the rest is dross," says poet Ezra Pound, and I am testing that proposition carefully, because my overall experience is that the basic fact of human life is loss. You lose everything, quickly or slowly, but finally. The things you hold on tightest to are ruined by the very panic of your grip. But perhaps it is true that the things you give away, rather than having been torn from your fingers, endure . . . for a little while . . . in some form. Physical tokens are, of course, but doors of memory. I have nothing of the vole's, but I will remember the vole because I saw it while looking around the edge of the hawk's lost pinion. The Bay of Tralee lies four thousand miles away, but I remember the sound of the waves, the crying of gulls, the presence of those I loved there in the slanting rain, by holding smooth, cool rock in my hand. The emerald flashes all the greens of all the rolling hills I've loved.

The gloomiest of my contemporaries expect the whole world to go—the living part of it, anyway—presently in a cataclysm of extinction. All right. I am as ready as I can be. I pick up bits of shell, dried husks of flowers, cast-off feathers. I fold them in among photos and love letters, all such things as are passed from the world-making a shrine of remembrance, concentrating on it long enough, hard enough, that it too may be lost, the physical mementos may be lost, and the inner world remain whole.

What thou lovest well remains. We shall see.

Midnight Sun

I KNOW I'M ON RECORD as saying I've never been to a real wilderness and that I don't care. But I was wrong. I have been to Alaska. And I do care. If the world was once like this, I am suddenly a radical and an activist. I want it back.

In the Bush Airport, Houston, there's a bronze statue of George Bush Sr., with his bronze coat flying behind him in the imaginary wind. I'm trying to locate the image in the glossary of Western art. It's the same pose as the Winged Victory of Samothrace, but, somehow, the impression left behind is quite different. It's like a contemporary businessman masquerading, for reasons that might once have seemed good, as Zeus. The classical drag is just not working. I want to draw a curtain, so that only certain people in a certain mood will have to see it. I want to stand behind the thing and keep it from tipping from its own ill-conceived distribution of bronze. I wish the expression on the president's face was less like a monster just risen from molten metal to lay waste to the world.

They have a joke in Alaska. They say if the Texans get too uppity, they'll divide Alaska in half and Texas will be only the third largest state.

It took me longer to fly to Anchorage from Houston than to Dublin from Atlanta. This gives a new sense of the scale of my own continent. Perhaps it's a horrifying sense, actually, for though such expanse is almost acceptable over the sea, over rock and tree it is too much.

When the plane emerges out of the highest cloud, what I see below is a wilderness of jagged mountains, snow-capped, with emerald valleys rolling upward, the vegetable green paling until it becomes the black of naked rock and then the streaked glare of the snowcaps themselves. The zones of vegetation are drawn as though on a schematic. The tree line is as sharp as the slash of a sword. Here and there the whiteness expands into vast glaciers, like mist lying between the mountains, but only a little less solid than the mountains themselves. The glaciers are torn with slashes of vibrant, unnatural aqua; crevasses, or perhaps optical illusions; and at the edge of the ice, swift streams burrow through the valleys or hurl into the fjords, the feathering brown of their silt tunneling far out into the green seawater with the energy of descent. To see a little of this would be impressive. To see it go on for miles and miles, as far as one can see from an airplane in any direction, except toward the sea, is sublimity off the human scale.

I'd have to live here a long time before I would begin thinking of this landscape as natural or ordinary. It looks like the mountain landscape that would be drawn by an imaginative child who has never see mountains, or by one of those "outsider" artists in whom naiveté is matched by an imbalanced mind. That it is beautiful cannot be said too often. That it is disturbing must be said at least once. I grew up in Ohio. For me the Smokies around Asheville, the Ox hills around Sligo count as real mountains. Here they would be foothills, if there were foothills before the sudden blue uprush of stone.

Jade green lakes spread from the edges of the glaciers. A jade green lake, pale and brilliant, may lie separated by no more than a narrow ridge of stone from one deep as malachite. I don't know what causes this. When the glacier ends at the sea, a whole bay or inlet becomes what looks like a lake of slush, calving icebergs at the edge. I am told there is a sound there like cannon fire.

The first few hours in Valdez, I spend turning round and round on the city street, trying to take in the periplum of rock and water, trying to reconcile to the bewildering asymmetry, the prodigal abundance of invention. No two mountains are the same; not one degree of horizon blends modestly into the next, but every inch a new creation, as though child titans were given stones and chisels and the general model of "mountain" and then left to do their work.

Bald eagles fly over Valdez harbor. While walking to the civic center I stop and listen to a yellow warbler. I ask him why he would live here when he could live in Carolina, but he won't stop singing long enough to answer. I hear thrushes in the underbrush. This, too, is disturbing, as though species I know were sown here just so the essential confoundedness might be intensified by occasional familiarity.

Anchorage now passes Edinburgh as the most northerly place I've stood on this planet. What must be mentioned is the clarity of the air, like Ireland's air, requiring less effort to get in and out of the lungs. The bright gashes on the mountains are waterfalls. The dark birds, sometimes harried by gulls, are eagles. I say these things to make myself easy with them. I look for the cages from which the stage-prop eagles have been released, but, of course, there are none.

I didn't know how I would react to the midnight sun. Turns out it makes me exultant and hilarious. To wake at 3 A.M. and be able to take a walk in a red twilight is a glorious thing. I think there must be animals not talked about, animals sprung from and inhabiting the queer, unfailing gleam, gryphons and centaurs that take their energy from the shimmering atmosphere. I can sleep fine in the light, even in the afternoons back home. The night's sleep is a luxurious catnap, full of dreams, the gulls crying over the masts in the harbor.

Beside the harbor. An Indian in a black shirt is playing a double flute at a picnic table, sweet, minor, haunting, piping for the mountain gods. The daisies are a snow beneath the snow.

Found a kindred soul, Matt Di Cintio, a playwright from Minneapolis. We met Dulcey Boehle at a fish fry. She is an Alaskan, not native, but of long enough standing to impress us. She was in the mood for a drive, so she took Matt and me down the Anchorage Road to see Bridal Veil Falls and Blueberry Lake (where her husband had proposed) and then to a glacier. The road was lined with purple lupine and scarlet fireweed. Dulcey observed that the glacier had receded hundreds of feet in her remembrance. All, deep into night, was still pervaded by that flat, unnatural perfection of blue sky, the limpid air, the jagged, bewildering particularity of every inch of the horizon. I longed to see moose or bear, but we saw none. It might have been too much if we had.

This is the longest day of the year, though where it is never dark, I wonder if that matters. Graffiti on a picnic table near the Valdez Civic Center: "Some people say that vandalism is as beautiful as a rock in a cop's face." The civic center grounds are decorated with great pots of petunias, pink, purple, magenta, white. They seem right for an indelicate landscape, horsey and aggressive, the fattest bee hardly causing a nod.

When I rose yesterday I hiked Valdez, pursuing the Dock Side Trail around its green peninsula, which took me, among other places, to a "Boreal Temperate Rain Forest."

121

All was shadowy and ferny and lush, with a deep cool preserved from the world before this world. The acres of mudflats upon which a sign promised me myriads of ducks sported not one duck. On the dock, the Indian was back, in his black shirt, blowing on the double flute. I don't think it was just the conjunction of the sea arm and the gleaming mountains with the music that made it so sweet. I think the man with the long ponytail was one of the great musicians of the world, and that he had been playing to the gods of the mountains, and they had been listening. I sat down beside him. I could feel the heat of his body, but I don't think he knew I was there until he had taken the flute from his mouth and I spoke to him.

Matt and I, to celebrate the solstice, got on board a Stephens cruise boat and sailed around Prince William Sound. Blistering sunburn is what I have to show for it now. Who would have thought to bring sunblock to Alaska? It is difficult now to know what to say about the cruise. The temptation is to get arithmetical and merely name the sights, the glaciers coming down to spend their white and cobalt in the silver water, the tortured crystal sculpture of the icebergs, the eagles and murres and puffins, the Stellar's sea lions and sea otters and the harbor seals, the sharks and the two great minke whales that fed miles from each other in lonely grandeur, the countless miles of the Chugach Range eaten by innumerable fjords coated by trees and haunted by beasts—it was the horrifying, transcendent expanse of the elder world that we built our cities first to punctuate and then to overpower.

It was at last crushed by it. I could endure not one more sublimity.

Now on a picnic table on the bluff overlooking the civic center, a high point overlooking all Valdez, I see a little whale surface and blow out in the fjord. I wonder if I'm the only one to see him. A porpoise, maybe, except he is too big and delays his flukes behind as a whale does. The hilltop is draped in fireweed. In a moment the flies will drive me down. Brilliant days—or I should say one brilliant day scarcely punctuated by a pale sickle moon and a silvery twilight—continue.

I sat in a blaze of light on the hill overlooking the civic center and began a play, about the whale and the flies and the unexpected hermit thrushes.

I'm trying to develop context for my experience here. I'm trying to find a way to understand an alien immensity. I find myself peering into ditches, counting the petals on wild flowers, following the progress of crawling insects, to focus on something of endurable proportions. The ducks in the Valdez harbor are fine. The gulls picking at the slurry of the fishing boats I understand. The straight fall of the waters from the sides of the mountain I cannot find a place for, or an eagle arrowing over my head as though it were a sparrow or a crow. A glacier, the green pools against the sides of glaciers, the glacier's edge where it shatters itself with a great shout into the sea, I have no categories for. Even the great works of man, cathedrals and symphonies and altar pieces, are works of man and therefore intelligible in kind, if not quite in degree. But I don't know whom to blame for this. Even the God I was used to doesn't work this way.

A curtain of light closes over Prince William Sound. The noon fire has become the twilight fire, and still I must angle my flat hand over my eyes. Last night as I left Matt in his room, the half moon stood in a sea of flawless turquoise, neither night nor day. I must bend my head and keep writing, if only to find some defense against the unrelenting tide of rock and sea and fire.

THE CHUGACH RANGE FROM THE AIR makes things clear. This is what the gods see from their hidden ramparts, a colossal simplicity of rock, snow, ice, of blue crevasses, of cold pale lakes, blue ice in a green sea, only the whales moving upon it. This is how the gods think of the world. To them it is immense, but so simple after all that a child—were he a god—could hold the guide ropes in his hands.

From the ground, where I am, it is more difficult. Around me are the million blue contours of the lupine. Over there is a horizon remade at every inch, jag following crag, crack succeeding craze, patternless, or with a pattern my mind will not grasp today, or tomorrow, or ever. The snow lies in ragged, dazzling blankets. The waterfalls leap from the high places and spread themselves into myriad-sided spray. Gull down floats from the gull's wing to float upon the crisscross chop of waters.

I sometimes think that my task is to remind God of the complexities, to remind the pantheon that some of us cannot move worlds by the tugging of a rein. We can scarcely move ourselves. We can barely understand the voice that wakes us to the throng of things, even when it is our own. Those of us who manage to speak are silent for a long time afterward, astounded by our daring, confounded by the echoes which will not cease—answering or refuting, we are not sure.

A Downtown Bestiary

I THINK IT'S A MERLIN, though the other merlins I've seen were by the sea near Portsmouth, New Hampshire—anyway, a little grayish falcon, the tail, which is mostly what I can see from the ground, boldly striped. It perches on the utility pole outside my studio, surveying the world of air and rail line and nearby river with an attitude as unlike the pigeons'—which resemble it in size—as a Marine's is unlike that of a used-car salesman. The resident mockingbirds flutter up and harass it, but it doesn't seem particularly perturbed. With what I imagine to be a shrug of its shoulders it arrows off to a pole not so near the mockingbirds, maybe closer to the river, where the hunting is better anyway. I allow myself to think it is visiting me. One of my studio mates is a skilled birdwatcher, and he has never seen the hawk, and though he doesn't call me a liar, I can see in his eyes that he doesn't believe—or perhaps resents—this special and particular visitation.

A SMALL BLACK BEAR wanders onto the grounds of the Cathedral of All Souls in Biltmore. It's not easy to decide where it has come from, though Biltmore does adjoin the vast Biltmore Estate and the Biltmore Estate adjoins the Blue Ridge Parkway. The bear wanders happily through the garth and flowerplots, and then, when startled by people, climbs up the drainpipes to the roof. There it stays while worried humans chatter on the wet lawns below. When night comes, the humans lose the black body of the bear in the black body of the night, and by morning it is gone, having negotiated four or five busy streets, having managed to be, apparently, invisible going both to and fro.

ALDER POND, AKRON, OHIO. Dawn came gray, except in the west, which was divided by a rainbow. The rainbow appeared as soon as the light did, as though it had been waiting in the dark. There must have been night rain. I don't remember.

TEN GEESE WERE GATHERED on the shore, ten smallish Canadas, in five obvious pairs. I'm used to Canadas being bigger than this. Perhaps they are stunted by the size of the

lake; perhaps only small ones come here, the flocks judging the bounty of the area from the air as they pass or descend. One pair is distinctly smaller then the others, their
feathers with a brownish cast, though still, one would say,
black and gray. I think the female is ill or hurt. She sits on
the ground, and when another bird approaches her, she
rises and lowers her neck in attack posture. None of the
others are afraid of her. They neither retreat nor attack
when she comes at them with her posture of fury. I think
the expression in their black eyes is pity.

Though they know I am there, the geese are all looking
out over the pond, as if expecting something, or, like me,
watching the water go from gray to gray gold to flashing gold
with the sun at the far rim. The biggest male honks and
flaps, then launches himself out over the lake. He makes a
flying tour above the brightening waters, then doubles back
and lands on the spot he just left. A few minutes pass. He
is still agitated over something. He and his mate swim out
into the water, fast at first, then slowing and looking about,
as people do when they have forgotten the purpose of the
journey. One of the left-behind geese begins to honk after
them. They stop, turn, paddle slowly back, as if summoned
to some sad duty they had almost escaped.

The impression the geese confab gives is of extreme
sociability, a complex society whose signals and concerns
are on one level perfectly plain, and on another, the profoundest mystery. They know what they are talking about,
and I know they are talking about something. Far away in
the hidden channels across the pond, there is a sudden

great splashing and honking. Then there is silence. The geese and I wait for the outcome, for great wings to break into the air or gray bodies to launch themselves over the gray water. But nothing happens. We all stare. Then, one by one, the geese slide into the water, heading for the invisible reed passages still wrapped in shadow.

BEAVER LAKE, ASHEVILLE. A mixed flock of geese, Canadas, Embdens, joined with mallards and even the occasional coot, cluster at the corner of Lakeshore Drive. It is a busy thoroughfare, down which impatient people make their way from place to place. But on any morning, on any afternoon, the traffic grinds to a halt while some fat Embden, some wary Canada with her line of goslings, cross the street in stately progress, from the green lawns to the receiving gray bosom of the lake.

FROM MY BEDROOM three stories over Sligo, on the west coast of Ireland, I can see the holy mountain Knocknarea, when it's not raining or there's no mist up from the sea. I could see the street, the outdoor market, and the great church of the Immaculate Conception before someone put up a looming block of flats. Still untouched by improvements stands the slant slate roof of McGettigan's Pub, festooned with pink and lavender cranny flowers, a gray, sky-dividing chimney, and the red iron landing of a fire escape, in case the whole shebang should go up in flames. I have forgotten how the custom started, but every night my last stop, after closing the pubs, is a little shop at the mouth of Connally Street, where I buy bread, crisps, day-old rolls. Though some few morsels may comprise a midnight snack for me, most of it I never intend to eat. I break the food into bite-sized pieces and drop them out the window onto the fire-escape landing. This must be done with the room lights turned off, for McGettigan's patrons are staggering to their cars about then, and if they looked up they would see me sowing the wind with bread, and what could be said in my defense? I sleep with the blankets drawn around me in the freezing room. At morning, then, sometimes before first light, sometimes just after, I'll hear a tapping of beak and talon on the metal of the fire-escape landing, and that will be the birds landing to harvest their offering, at once my alarm clock and the best possible doorway to a new day.

131

Jackdaws and crows are the most abundant visitors, the crows looming enormous and a little frightening in the tiny window, their cries—of derision, I suppose, at the paucity of the offering—must wake the whole house. When I put a picked-over chicken carcass out, or if I repeat the ritual in full daylight, great white gulls soar in from the sea, driving other birds away by the power of sheer majesty, scrunching up on the fire escape like huddling ghosts. Once there was an owl. He was not interested in the bread, but he was in the birds that ate it, and there was silence on my fire-escape landing until she eased away under the roof of McGettigan's garage.

For some reason I do not apply the term "scavengers" to these airy Irish visitors, though by any objective account, that's what they are. I do apply that word to creatures coming to a similar feast under the identical impulse back home in Carolina: sparrows and pigeons and rats, too familiar, maybe, for the same degree of affection. When I had a business downtown, on Patton Avenue, I knew when the rats would come out of the drain gratings and congregate like idle citizens on the street. I would leave late sometimes, just to see them. They were calm and happy and could be approached quite closely. This emergence was the sign that the reign of men downtown was over for the night, and the reign of wild things was beginning. My gallery was a pioneer on lower Patton, and at first the rats would emerge to their forays at ten or eleven because there were no people to challenge them. By the time I was moving out, so were the rats. A bar had opened beside me, and there was pedestrian traffic until past two. That was already past my bedtime, so I don't know when the rats started hitting the streets, but it must have been the beginning of lean times, unless the bounty provided by restaurant and bar made up for the curtailed gleaning time.

Why it should be that Sligo's scavengers come from the air and Asheville's, for the most part, from the ground, was a puzzle until I considered that Ireland, beautiful as it is, is a disaster zone in terms of biodiversity. A little island in the first place, not fully repopulated after the retreat of the glaciers and before the rising of the sea (which is why there are no snakes there, whatever claims are made for Saint Patrick), it has undergone seven hundred years of the most rapacious misuse by a wasteful colonial power and, consequently, by its own desperate people. After the glaciers, nothing big and wild remained but a scattering of deer. Anything that hugged the ground with four feet was practically wiped out. But the air and the water provided some sanctuary. If you stand on the Sligo quays you can see the salmon heading for the Garravogue practically fin to fin, boiling the shallows like something out of old legend, great hunching herons on the far bank waiting for their fill. The air swirls with birds at dusk and at morning. Sligo Strand is a paradise with the center, the dry land, unpeopled.

But in Asheville I live pretty well in the interior of a giant continent, and nothing but humanity keeps bison and grizzly and jaguar from walking over my flower beds. The local news brightens every now and then with stories of black bears wandered into suburbs. For a season or two there were almost daily media updates on the falcon that had set up housekeeping in the BB&T bank, our tallest building not so unlike a shining black mesa. Traffic stopped, bistro diners let their forks hover in midair when the slender, swift figure zoomed between buildings on Pack Square. It was sensational. If I could figure out how it was arranged, I would believe it was a setup by the chamber of commerce.

At one point a trim young man, Ukiah Morrison, began walking around downtown Asheville clothed in nothing but a G-string—which turns out, surprisingly, to be quite legal.

"Private parts" must be covered in public, of course, but buttocks turn out not to be included in the statute denominating private parts, so Ukiah was home free. Morrison ran for city council and was featured in a May 2000 issue of *Rolling Stone* as an element that helped make our little mountain town the new "Freak Capital" of America. If *that* had been a covert chamber of commerce stunt, the "freak capital" thing must have seemed a bit of a backfire for the upright restauranteurs and shopkeepers of the city center.

For a while we locals divided into those who had seen Ukiah in the almost altogether, and those who had yet to experience that pleasure. Interestingly, the media coverage—sorry—of Ukiah Morrison was all but indistinguishable from the coverage of the falcon. In both cases, there were excitedly documented sightings. There were prophecy and analysis. There was raffish joy. There was worry: some wanted the falcon to go away lest enviro-Nazis used its presence as a way to compromise property rights; some wanted Morrison to go away . . . well, I suppose because the whole thing was pretty weird; but also, undeniably, because while people were gawking at Ukiah or the falcon, they weren't buying anything. Both wonders had momentarily stopped the wheels of daily life. People looked up from their ordinary business to say "Oh!"

There were some who thought of each, therefore, as a divine visitation.

While the peregrine was getting the media focus, a very young red-shouldered hawk was living downtown, too, practicing her hunting skills at the edge of the YMCA parking lot. I was there when she tumbled heavily from the sky onto the grassy slope between the Y and First Baptist and in two pounces had finished off a pigeon. I didn't know whether to look and risk drawing a crowd, which might spook or harm her, or turn away and miss something you don't see every day. I stayed and watched, and a crowd did gather, of excited fathers and sons, mothers and daughters, who neither spooked nor harmed the young huntress. The hawk seemed indifferent to us, already a seasoned urbanite, going about the business of a kill with the exaggerated correctness of the tyro, deigning to notice enough to mantle her prey—lifting her wings in such a way that we were not supposed to be able to make out what she was doing—in case we had a mind to steal it from her.

A sharp-shinned hawk covered my own front yard with bloody feathers for a while, apparently holing up in the neighbor's spruce and launching at the local birds as they drank or splashed in my birdbath. I never saw the hunter, except for once, as a great shadow I inadvertently frightened from its mark by walking onto the porch. My neighbor saw it and described it, which is why I think it was a sharp-shin. But I did see the piles of bloody feathers it left behind, crushed and fanned out in a circle, as though a bomb had been dropped on jays and robins from a passing plane.

My birdbath, like a watering hole in an African savannah, gives richness to my suburban biota. The first birdbath I had was faux-marble plastic, and it was puzzling why it should be empty in the morning, even if I had filled it the night before. I had seen dogs drinking from it—you had to be a pretty tall dog to do so—but even their doggy gulps weren't enough to change the water level appreciably. One night I was having a party, which meant that an unusual number of people were outside unusually late at night, with the porch lights on. It was cool, and mostly smokers congregated outside where they could light up in peace. From inside with my other guests, I heard a loud murmur out on the porch. I went to investigate. There were two young raccoons by the birdbath. One was standing on his hind legs. His front claws were hooked onto the rim of the birdbath. When he was smaller, this was probably his method to hoist himself up for a drink, but now he was big enough to bend the plastic rim and bring the water cascading down on his upturned muzzle, a sensation which he obviously enjoyed. His sister lapped the water he spilled on the stone flags around them.

I had cooked a large turkey for the crowd. It was I, I'm ashamed to say, who conceived the idea of feeding the raccoons. They looked so young, so vulnerable. We brought the picked-over turkey carcass out and began hand feeding the little creatures. It seemed the right thing to do, even if it was amusing at the same time. Where was their mother? Which of the bloating roadkills along Lakeshore Drive had once been her? They walked fearlessly up the stairs to us, took meat and bone from our hands with their little hands, neither pushy nor obsequious, but perfect guests. Even when the raccoon kits were no longer hungry, they were

136

curious. They were having a good time at the party, and though they were not the last guests to leave for home, they were by no means the first.

The raccoon kits were with me most of the summer. I saw them nudge under tiles on my neighbors' roof before dawn, probably living in their attic, getting back to their nest through a breach in the seam of a gable. One night, heading downtown, I looked back for some reason and saw a large, amorphous shape clinging to one of my porch pillars. It was a strange mass, moving on the pillar in an unintelligible, terrifying way, and I seriously considered the possibility of some gelatinous alien intruder before the mass broke in two and half tumbled to the ground, leaving the other half in the unmistakable shape of a baby raccoon.

I liked having them. They were wild and went away to sleep and eat, yet behaved otherwise like pets: the best of both worlds. I handled it badly, but who could blame me? One night the young raccoons simply were not there. I pushed the worst and likeliest explanations out of my head and mapped in my imagination possible routes to large forested areas: across backyards and the deadly barrier of Merrimon Avenue to Beaver Dam and the Blue Ridge Parkway . . . down wooded avenues to the valley of the French Broad . . . straight north to the farms of Weaverville. . . . Two clever raccoons could make their way anywhere if they wanted, given just a few breaks. It is not impossible, either, that the coming wisdom of maturity taught them to go invisible even among former friends

137

and that they are still with us, and the cocking of my cat's head in the middle of the night is at the sound of them scuffling in my crawl space, that the ripped garbage bags people blame on somebody else's dogs are not the work of dogs at all. An enormous opossum rooted around on my terrace at night all last summer, and I couldn't imagine where he spent his days hidden—it would be like hiding a collie—and if a stupid marsupial could make that happen so could my cunning friends.

Down around my studio, between the railroad tracks and the French Broad River, lies a wilderness, very narrow but very wild. Blue-tailed skink haunt the front doorway, all those bricks sun warmed on a western wall, all those high grasses teeming with bugs. Ducks land on the river daily, some arriving at dawn, others at twilight from God knows where. Geese, big pushy Canadas, contest with dogs the rulership of junkyards and rail right-of-ways and the shady deserts under bridge supports. What crawls in and out of the riverside crawl spaces I don't even want to know. Bats, like pigeons and squirrels and sparrows, are so numerous and common they hardly count as "wild" animals anymore, but as neighbors, urban and hospitable, quiet, night workers whom one sees mostly going to or coming home from their jobs. The great greenish light that lights our parking lot spreads a banquet table in the middle of the air.

EVERY NOW AND THEN there will be a change in the chattering of the birds outside my studio window, which heralds the appearance of the resident hawk. One can hear the heavier tink of his claws on the railing of the metal fire stairs. One can hear the indignation and panic in the voices of his prey. He is difficult to see, what with the close quarters and plenty of places to hide, but I have run out to the fire landing quickly enough to see a proud shadow, blunt winged and, even to me, terrifying, sweeping back over the metal roof. I would put something out on the fire escape for him if I could think what it would be.

We do also, of course, have a resident studio mouse, a handsome brown specimen, bright eyed and no more frightened than he needs to be. No skulker in corners he. If our mouse if not intimidated, neither is he very intimidating—at this point I am the only one who has seen him—so he is not the explanation for why nobody likes to be at the studio alone at night. The place is just across from the river, on the other side of which are the acres of the Biltmore Estate and, beyond that, the Blue Ridge Parkway stretching away to the north and south into the mountains. Anything might swim over in the night and lurk among the boxes and old machines, waiting for things to get quiet.

I hope so, anyway.

We are not again likely, for a very long time, to live in a world where the rhinos and the bears and the great hunting cats are actual neighbors. We could begin to make do with what we have. Beside that, beside the woodchucks and the half-tame ducks and the cartoonish rodents that serve as inhabitants of our wild kingdom, we are creating a biota specifically to dwell with us. Many creatures are, simply put, our invention: my three big black cats are things that nature would never have thought of; the domestic dog, most of the farm animals, hosts of pigeons and rabbits and fowl are ours, and at least some of them have a chance of making it once our husbandry is at an end. I'm betting on my cats, anyway. The Elisha Mitchell Audubon Society here in town maintains that hundreds of millions of songbirds are killed each year by feral cats. I don't know how such data is gathered, but neither do I doubt it. Mice wander into the house in bitterest winter, and the speed of their dispatch by my cats—big, fat, lazy, with no possible previous hunting experience—is nothing short of electrifying.

In more subtle ways, it is reasonable to think that we have influenced the evolution of rats and squirrels and flies and swallows and rat-eating snakes and yard grasses and creatures that eat yard grasses in ways we might never fully comprehend. Pigeons, starlings, sparrows, the black rat, though perfectly natural creatures, were not intended by nature to inhabit the vast expanses of North America they now fill. The white-tailed deer is bewildered by the bountiful new menu set out by suburban landscapers. We are creating— perhaps have created—the next world. The Patton Avenue rats adjusted their schedules to harmonize with ours. The studio woodchuck knew exactly when to put in an appearance so as to coax a morsel or two from the noisy apes.

Armadillos get clobbered on the highways not merely because they are stupid, but because they have a reflex to jump into the air when startled—a pretty good strategy with a fox or a wolf, but suicide under the chassis of a truck. Deer, foxes, raccoons, other sorts of creatures, which are not, relatively speaking, stupid at all, still get mesmerized by headlights, something nothing in ten million years of evolution equipped them for. When the holocaust is over, when all the creatures we can kill have been killed, when the creatures that live off us without our fully knowing have taken what they can, it will be interesting to see who's left. It will be still more interesting to see *why* they're left: those, perhaps, with an impulse to turn away from sudden bright light and run in the other direction; those who live on sewage and disdain response to petrochemicals; those who relish the din and clutter of cities; those who learned to love tunnels and roads and the dark beneath them; those who like us, or fear us wisely, who are cute and cuddly, or so stealthy we were never sure they were there. Biologists millions of years hence will look at some behaviors and wonder where on earth *that* came from . . . that taste for vertical surfaces, that longing for the hard and shiny, that fearless begging, that ingratiating tail wag. Maybe someone will be left to say, "It was we. We wanted them that way, and there they are." I don't find this particularly distressing or too far from the normal operation of the planet. What but the stalking leopard made us stand upright on the plain? What but the circling monkey eagle put it into our heads to chatter, "There! There!"

WOLFEN is a stylish fantasy horror film from 1981, starring Albert Finney, which postulates a tribe of magical wolves inhabiting the inner city, feeding off the wandering

scum of the human race. They are so cunning or so en-
chanted as to be all but invisible, and so subtle as hunters that they pick off only those who will not be missed.
Though I acknowledge that the concept of people who will
not be missed is problematic, the film is fascinating, and
has dwelt in my imagination enough that I bought my
own copy and view it every so often. That we should at
length acquire our own breed of predators—above the
level of flukes and bacteria—seems not very far-fetched,
and even, in a way, beautiful. Whatever uses we put being
swift-of-foot or keen-of-eye or quick-of-thought to in
the fullness of time, we must acknowledge that the original
use was to flee, or to catch what fled. The greatest beauty
and the greatest hazard lie side-by-side. Someday we may
set aside our present obsession with safety and prize again
the beauty or the valor or the cunning or the daring that
delighted our ancestors while they danced on the edge
of personal oblivion. Something watching with bright eyes
from the shadows, something almost now our match, which
we ourselves created by living the way we live, could but raise
all bars.

At the Millennium

I DON'T EVEN KNOW WHAT TO CALL THIS PLACE. If you pull off the Blue Ridge Parkway at Bent Creek Gap, park your truck just outside the echoing stone bridge, and head to the right, down toward Bent Creek, you're on the road that leads to it. Half an hour's walk from the truck, a steep road leaps off to the right from behind a swinging gate. At the end of that weedy road lies one of the sacred places.

Brilliant winter sun blasting through the leafless forest makes seeing difficult—a Miltonic oxymoron, blind from excess of light. You must turn away from anything directly in the light and glance with the sides of your eyes. Not that there's that much to look at, fauna-wise. It is New Year's morning, after all, and the wildlife too must be sleeping it off. Not a bird. Not a chattering squirrel. There are two sounds: the sweet, springlike wind, and the sound of my nylon jacket rubbing against itself as I move. I stop to listen to the wind, which is really a kind of silence. In spaces between the wind, the quiet is so deep it pulsates, like some dark heart beating at the bottom of the valley.

The road is shorter than I remember it. This perception is important, for it is a day dedicated to the passage of time, and I have always thought that ways must lengthen and grow wearisome as one ages. Not this one, not yet. When I enter the great tilted meadow, I realize fully that it is early morning of the first day of the third millennium after Christ, and that it is likely—no, necessary—that I am the first man to step into the place in this age, and, as all slates are wiped clean, all ledgers balanced at the stroke of midnight, that makes me a discoverer.

I move down the meadow, along the left side, the sunrise side, until I find a patch of forest to hunker down in, a patch with dry leaves and a clear view of Mount Pisgah, six crow miles further to the southwest. I ask myself what is the one word to capture the mountain this morning. Majestic? Aloof? Steely? Oddly enough, the word would be "poised." In the supernaturally clear light, the mountain seems leaning, off balance, as though it were gathering itself for some titanic leap. Poised for flight, as the saying goes. Behind the blue gray mass glide the only clouds in the sky. It is as if they were being born and escaping from a great womb in the heart of the stone. The hills that climb toward the summit are marvelous but appreciably smaller than the dark Aztec pyramid of Pisgah proper. Abstract the television tower on the peak, and it is anyone's idea of the sacred mount.

The sweet clemency of the day—the January day four thousand feet up in the Blue Ridge—is almost impossible to credit. Again abstracting the transmission tower—and maybe adding a few trees to the meadow, which must be at least in part man-made—Pisgah would likely not look much different, or visibly different at all if I were sitting on this spot on January I, 1001—with the West divided between the Emperor in Byzantium and the Caliph in Cordova; while the Vikings, turned Normans, were making their final and most lasting inroads; while my heroic ancestors were grudgingly cohabiting with the yellow-haired invaders in their new town of Dublin beside the Black Pool. Were one to return in a thousand years, would the eye detect a difference? Barring, maybe, China, no nation that was on earth in 1000 is recognizable in 2000. One has little reason to doubt the same will be true in the other direction. Meanwhile, upon the sacred mountain, a rock slide alters the contour of a slope a decade or two until the scar is re-covered by trees. Nobody, from this distance, would have noticed anyway. If the feel of the mountain this morning is kinetic, is a vibrant potential, it has been this way for a thousand millennia, taut as a drawn bow, quivering, never released. On the last day, if ever comes such a day, what shaft is finally launched from it will pierce the heavens.

The atmosphere whispers *sleep*. I fight off drowsiness for a while, then ask myself why. There is no reason not to do what the wind says. Sleep. Sleep. I arrange my jacket, slip my knapsack under my head, and slide into unconsciousness.

I wake suddenly—who knows why? There are more clouds now, and the wind is fresher. I have chosen as my lair a space, one end of which is formed by a single white pine in a grove of mostly maples. The bark of the pine in the clear light—like a poured crystal congealing on the mountains—possesses a variety of colors and textures, a sensual abundance almost literally beyond description. For some reason, contemplation of the tree puts me in a geometrical humor. What would one do were one charged with measuring the actual surface of this planet, a total of which must include every ridge and bump, the expanse of the walls of every crack and delve, the area of every tunnel of the borers, every scallop of the chewed twig, and all that on just this one stunted pine. Would such a surface, drawn into a line, stretch to Jupiter? To the next star? As I paddle around in these thoughts, I become aware that there is a sound behind me unlike the rattle of branches or the random scrape of dry leaves.

It is an animal. Quite near.

Is it human? No. Far too irregular. Softer.

I sit bolt upright, turning around with a motion that I hope will not prove startling to whatever is there. I am now muzzle to muzzle with a skunk. If you put one end of a yardstick on my nose, the other could rest easily on his. The skunk's black mask is drawn tightly over the little skull, the tiny black weasel eyes watchful but not especially alarmed. For some reason, his countenance strikes me as the drollest thing on earth, and I grin broadly, hoping the skunk has some talent at reading human physiognomy. Whatever he registers from me, I gather from him a shallow fringe of curiosity edging a profundity of indifference. I do have food in my knapsack, two Christmas tangerines, but citrus is not usually a hit with wild animals. I realize that what brought him here out of all the forest round is less likely me than the same features that attracted me: a dry mound, well sunned, good visibility, very slightly higher than the surrounding ground, though still plenty of undulations to get lost in, especially if one were two feet long. I have already slipped two discarded plastic soda bottles into my knapsack, one clearly older than the other, attesting to the fact that *Homo sapiens* have been drawn to this spot before—in another millennium, though hardly worth thinking about now.

My little friend waddles past my right shoulder. He fills the space with the odor of tranquil skunk, something one would hardly call subtle, but not at all unpleasant, and, to me, slightly arousing. He pads boldly out to the edge of the meadow, where, like a child crossing a busy road, he looks carefully both ways, sniffs the air, and tumbles on through the frostbitten weeds. His held-high rear end (proudly exhibiting the small but no doubt mighty testes which embolden me to say "he" through all this) is still visible when a rifle crack sounds out on the slope below the meadow. This explains the skunk's uncustomary mid-day hegira. There's another rifle crack, quite close, but far enough below the brow of the hill that neither my skunk buddy nor I sense danger. I stand up, thinking that my whole body will look less like a squirrel than just the reddish crown of my head bobbing over a leafy mound. I'm still standing, peeling and eating a tangerine, when a hunter emerges from thickets at the bottom of the meadow. The skunk is still visible, like a ship at distance, vanishing slowly over the crown of the hill. There is no such thing as skunk season. He knows it.

I do not have the attitude toward hunting that most people assume I will. Maybe if I had run into more goof-ball hunters I would think differently, but all the hunters I have encountered in the woods have been responsible, sober, even grave, as though they had taken solemnity from the imperial solemnity of the mountains. I do not think that hunting, done with respect, is immoral. There is a mysticism about it as old as humankind, a masculine mystery cult not to be condemned lightly. At best, hunting is deep ecology's deepest ally. Contemporary paganism is an invention of the last century (which is to say, the twentieth), and though it has made a good start on revaluing the natural world, its traditions are broken from the past, artificial, and often silly. Yes, high-powered rifles, etc., are an embarrassment to the spirit, but for the moment, the hunt is what we retain from the deep past of humanity on Terra.

Those who used to be a priesthood are now conceived of as a battalion of marginals trickling from the trailer parks into the woods in their crisp camo of a Saturday morning. I do not contend this picture is untrue; merely that it is not the whole story. Hunter, in any case, and environmentalist are natural allies. Nothing worse can be conceived for the environmental movement than that these two wilderness-loving factions should find themselves at odds. Maybe in this century, the pagans, the hunters, the earnest-eyed kids over in the university environmental science labs, a handful of the religious who remember a God who is the creator and sustainer of the natural world, will form an alliance to shake the counsels of power.

Anyway, as this particular hunter came toward me he was revealed gradually to be a dark-haired, beefy kid of about twenty-five (I have taken to calling anyone under thirty "kid").

"Squirrels?" I say

"Yep. Seen any?"

I allowed as how I had not.

The kid told me about where he had been that day, the long loop he had made in the shadow of Pisgah in order to wind up at that spot at an hour when he knew it would be "pretty." I keep my conviction that it is my meadow to myself. He told me that in deer season that meadow—part of whose attraction is that it's a perfect deer habitat—would have seven or eight hunters hidden in cover at the sides.

"How do they keep from blasting each other to pieces?"

"Hell, the deer know they're here. They never see a deer. They never fire a shot."

Just like the squirrels, I thought, on this strangely silent hunting day.

The hunter continued toward the high end of the meadow. He had not fired the shots I heard, so there were others close about. My mood was broken—in good time, actually—and I still had a New Year's party to clean up after, so I made for the road out. I heard at least two more hunters in the woods to my right. The day had become quite warm as it met and passed noon. I took off my jacket and my sweatshirt, which not only cooled me, but had the added advantage of revealing my T-shirt, which was bright red. I wouldn't have gone to the woods all dressed in woodsy green had I remembered it was squirrel season. I was a little nervous about the hunters, but didn't want to shout to them, lest it spook their quarry. Then one appeared on the road just in front of me. He was a red-haired giant, with a grinning, happy face that somewhat offset and somewhat completed his enormous stature and shining rifle. When I came close to him, before we had even said hello, he reached into his side pack and pulled out the body of a grouse that he had blasted so recently that its body was warm and supple. The rifle crack I had heard below the hill was the death of the bird.

"Young one. Pretty, ain't he?"

"You gonna cook him?"

"Yeah, nothing like grouse breast."

I do not hunt, and I couldn't quite fathom the man's

full emotion. Part of it was admiration. Part of it was—
well, something that saw no contradiction in killing what
you admire, that felt that the killing was part of the admiration. I didn't ask him to explain it. Figured it was one
of those things that explanation would always fail. The sun
was already declining. We were headed in opposite directions on the meadow road.

THE FRONT PLATE OF THE PICKUP parked beside mine at
the echoing bridge read "Mark 'n' Marie." I was betting
Mark was the dark-haired beefy hunter. I reached into my
knapsack for paper to leave him a note-but what would it
say? I have a revelation, reach back in the knapsack, and
complete the note, easing it under the windshield wiper.
"Happy Hunting," it said.

Happy Hunting.

A couple times a year I get it into my head to buy a gun.
Then I remember my temper and my melancholy and con-
clude that I remain better off without. Still, I am no enemy
of guns in the forest. They are like the claws and pointed
teeth on my sleeping, fat cats: the remembrance of something vital, the next need of which one cannot foresee.

THERE WAS A BIG FLURRY OF LIST MAKING at the end
of the millennium, who was the greatest person, what was
the most significant event, that sort of thing. Gutenberg's
moveable type won, as I remember, for the great achieve-
ment of the age, and it's not that I don't think that was
nifty, but that it seems to me more the crest of a long

slope, something already sufficiently provided for as to seem inevitable, something, furthermore, already developed by the Chinese. Plus, it would figure that we would light on something mechanical. I'd prefer something previously unimaginable, coming out of the air like a falling star. Something spiritual, if possible, a revelation. I might choose the discoveries of William Blake, taken as a coherent philosophy. Blake had a vision of each man as a towering giant, a fourfold angelic power, tripped up and made tiny by his own inner jealousies and the envy of a fallen world. Blake's great epic, *The Four Zoas,* tells the story of the fall of the giant Albion, of the growing and inexplicable imbalance in his soul, the jealousy between mind and feeling, after which all is chaos: intellect at war with the emotions, the emotions at war with the animal flesh, until Albion's faculties hate and fear each other, every emotion a threat to his mind, every thought a threat to his heart, every appetite a terror to his soul, and he falls and falls, shedding glories like some great lamp falling into the sea, until he reaches the Limits of Contraction, which is our present life. Albion, of course, is us, a god so long as he holds himself together, a squabbling manikin in the slough into which he has let himself descend. I don't know of anything that more aptly describes the frustrations—one daren't say "tragedies"—of the contemporary world. Change the names of Blake's warring gods to psychological terms and you have everybody nodding and murmuring, "Oh, yes."

Was Blake an environmentalist? I think he would think that if we were still angels and titans, we would not be

154

content to dwell anywhere but paradise. I think he would think the human soul needs the proper backdrop before which to engage its dramas. I think he would think that beauty is the only fit habitation for the redeemed soul. He was the one who wrote, "A robin redbreast in a cage / Puts all Heaven in a rage."

Could be that we might add a few verses of Ezra Pound to the millennial remembrance. Crystal rules his epic poem *The Cantos,* gods moving through crystal, goddesses and neglected daughters entering the great crystal, flames and hearts and solemn music wrapped in imperishable crystal. He is talking, of course, about the last flaw of all perfect earthly things, mutability, of the imagination's power to wrap them in crystal and preserve them forever. This idea has a special resonance here on the first day of the millennium, on the ridge of a mountain that is made of dark crystal laid upon dark crystal, under a dome of scintillant crystal fire.

I LISTEN FOR THE ECHO OF GUNS, but the crystal slopes are at peace. My guess is that the squirrels and my friend the skunk will have no memory of a morning of danger. Only much higher animals have any use for anxiety. The mountains again are sanctuary. I don't know what they're called, the visible hills, except the big one over there, except for Pisgah. Perhaps I should name them all anew for the millennium: the Angel, the Dinosaur, the Bride, the Blue Table. . . . Ideally you'd have different names for the same mountain, depending on where you were looking at it from, depending on the season, the time of day, what was blossoming in the cracks between its stone. Pisgah amid his brotherhood of sunlit hills makes me think of Blake's Albion, the eternal upright spirit, the blue giant striding among giants. All climb an endless stair into the crystalline fire.

This landscape is still new to me. I did not grow up in the mountains. They are not home yet; they are something still to notice, to accommodate, to scrutinize. I am still a tourist. Back where I grew up, the sky was the major natural feature, a whirling and rootless power, sunstruck and cyclone haunted, inspiration without a text, clouds and thunder and the varying light forever in motion. You could take to the heavens or you could stay rooted to the soil, but there was no intermediate choice. Here there is something else, another element, a stone road between heaven and earth. Here is Pisgah, motionless, even when the scurry of clouds and cloud shadows across his face almost looks as though he meant to budge—motionless, serene, authoritative, composed, vibrant with sleeping power. I would have been different had I grown up in his shadow. I would have been different had I grown up a mountaineer. I watch him from my nameless, squirrel-less, skunkblessed tilted meadow, wondering, on the first day of an age, what this age might come to. Pisgah has many more such ages to see even before he visibly changes his countenance. I will be gone in a heartbeat. Let me suck this one in like fine wine.

Nectar

THE PEACEFUL GARTH OF ALL SOULS CATHEDRAL in Asheville blooms with trumpet-shaped flowers. The ashes of the parish's dead are scattered there; perhaps that is the reason for the floral abundance. Now it's coffee hour after morning service, and I am holding a cup of coffee and talking with a boy, of, I think four or five. He will not come close to the flowers because they are alive with bumblebees, and he is afraid. I tell him he shouldn't be afraid, because no bee in the world has it in her mind to do him harm.

I move in toward the nicotiana, where fat bumblebees

wallow in white and lilac trumpets. I move my finger slowly toward one of them, compensating for the sway of the breeze. I touch the back of the bumblebee. I pet her, first softly, and then hard enough to bend her wings and let them spring back in the sunlight. She is so intent on her pollen that, once she feels I mean no harm, I am no more to her than a passing breeze. The boy stands peering over the nicotiana with a look of amazement in his eyes, of hero worship, which I did not intend, but which is gratifying nevertheless. He is touching the bee. He thinks I have done something magical, that the power to pet bees is in me rather than simply in the nature of things. I tell him how if he is very, very gentle and is not afraid, the bumblebees will be gentle and unafraid, too. I tell him not to try it with wasps or hornets, though I think it would probably work with them, too. Before coffee hour ends, his mother marches toward me, holding him in her arms as though he were hurt.

"Benny told me what you showed him. I hope you intend to be around to take care of him when he gets stung!" She is as angry as she dares to be at church. I think I have given her son a gift of fearlessness; she thinks I have tempted him to peril. The panic in his mother's voice has made Benny cry. I figure he will not soon pet the bees.

HORNETS DUG A BURROW and founded a nest beside my dead rose. They did this in a single day. Yesterday I weeded there and there was nothing, while today I watered and had to flee from a formation of angry hornets. I gave it a good deal of thought, but finally decided that a hornet's nest exactly there, which I must pass to use the hose, which I must use every day it doesn't rain, cannot be tolerated. I tried to hose them out, but that was a mistake. I don't know why I didn't get stung. So I filled a bucket with dirt and waited until late in the evening. I watched in the fading light as hornet after hornet went in, but no more came out. In the last purple gray of evening, when there had been no activity at the burrow's mouth for several minutes, I poured the dirt on the hole and then watered it, so that the dirt would turn to mud and fill all the chambers of the insects. I took no pleasure in this. I felt, in fact, as if I'd committed a desecration, though how I was to continue regular life without committing it I don't know. When I returned to the front door, I felt myself tearing a substantial spiderweb that had been spun in the space of half an hour between the rhododendrons. Tonight I thought I might go out for a walk, but as I went down the front steps, I caught in the faint gleam of light from the house the shadow of a spider hovering in the air—in the center of its invisible web, of course. I went back inside for a flashlight, and watched a great garden spider making a meal of a june bug. For the sake of the slaughtered hornets, I was going to inconvenience no more arthropods this night. I went back inside, letting the web stand until the morning until at least the weaver finished its meal. The web was beautiful. The spider made it faster than I could draw it.

I REMEMBER LOOKING AT A PIECE OF AMBER on a museum shelf, with a caption that explained that the body inside was a proto-ant, its relatives, even as it died in golden goo, involved in the process of transforming from their former existence as wasps. I had been stung by wasps and bitten by ants and the sensation was the same, acidic and infuriating; my creamy pink-white peonies will not open without the ministry of black, bitter ants, which seem to have spread the wasp's sting over their entire bodies. Suddenly it all makes sense: one tribe, part of which folded its wings and delved into the dirt.

I wonder if the fossil record shows as clearly by what progression came forth the bees and the flowers. Bees first: ready, willing, and able—"preadapted" is the evolutionary word—to service the flowers; or the flowers, haphazardly depending on wind, rain, beetles, what have you, until the right vector, that long-awaited creature known erewhile only to the mind of God, appeared?—or both at the same fortuitous moment, a biological Romeo and Juliet spotting each other in the midst of a party intended, so it seemed, for another crowd altogether? What is plain is that, in the midst of the reign of the dinosaurs, the plants did a strategic about-face. Prior to that time they had hidden their nutritious seeds behind spikes and walls and integuments, in the depths of cones, booby-trapped by bitter resins, where nobody but the very strong or the very specialized could reach them. The incipient angiosperms took a look at the situation and reasoned, "Well, if they're going to be at us all the time anyway, we might as well find a way to make use of it; we might as well embrace it." Thereupon they put forth a staggering array of drupes and pomes and berries and fruits, nuts and seeds and

samaras, great juicy feasts of sweet vegetable meat, precisely to attract the attention of animals, who would eat
the offerings, catching the seeds on their fur or foot pads
or in the hallways of their guts and trotting them off to new
lands inaccessible to the plants themselves.

The gymnosperms had already perfected the use of
armor, so it was no trouble producing a seed casing that
would pass merrily through the gut of a duckbill or an
orangutan. In some cases, the seeds *needed* such a passage,
usually through the grinding gizzard of a bird, to germi-
nate at all. Turkeys had to be introduced to the Mauritius
Islands, as the extinction of the dodo had signed the death
warrant of certain trees, which had grown so accustomed
to passing their seeds through the dodo's crop that they
could no longer reproduce otherwise. The extinction of
the passenger pigeon changed the face of the American
forest in more than one way, for many plants had used it
as a reproductive vector. Anyway, the strategy was prime:
blueberry puts forth fruit; triceratops comes by and thinks
"For me?" and eats; seeds of blueberry go wherever triceratops goes, until the digestive process is at an end and the
germination process begun.

It works just as well with a bear or a deer, of course, and
there is reason to believe that bear and deer—not to mention most of the other extant mammalian herbivores—
are the way they are largely because of the banquet table laid
by the angiosperms. The flowers and the beasts evolved to
take advantage of each other, actually create each other, in
the headiest atmosphere of cooperation in evolutionary

history: Here, say the flowers, here is the banquet laid for you! Take and eat!

Here, say the herbivores and the omnivores, *here is my fur, my muddy feet, my capacious gut and rich feces, my pants cuffs dragged through the grass. Trust me with your generations!*

Why should not this spirit enter into the making of the seeds as well as the dispersal of them? Before the delicious fruit, the angiosperms put forth delicious flowers, and out of the womb of time came the bees to wallow in them. Most gymnosperms spread their pollen by wind or water. Most angiosperms employ an animal vector—bees, bats, beetles, butterflies, certain specialized ground-dwelling mammals. It is an invitational, a community project. Nectar is nonfunctional except as a lure and a reward. The workings of my peculiar mind allow me to believe that the world puts forth beauty for the hell of it, but a more "scientific" view is that the whole splendor of the flowering planet is toward the completion of this enormous interchange.

If we think we're above it ourselves, we need only to think what would happen to us if the flowers—that is to say, everything from the grasses to the bananas and the oaks—were to fail. Spitting your watermelon seeds, blowing on a dandelion puff, pulling burrs off your sleeve, picking a strawberry seed from between your teeth, you're part of it, you're doing a job older and more intimate than any civilized vocation. A world based on mutual reward is not a bad one, I think; indeed, a very beautiful one, and one that restates a needful precept. I teach at a university, so I hear my share of philosophical conversations which rehash ancient controversies, partially because certain controversies are, by their nature, unresolvable, partially because the learning process involves simply hearing yourself think.

One chestnut is the notion that no one ever does anything out of utter altruism, that even the most self-immolating sacrifice is at least accompanied by a sense of satisfaction. Mostly this argument is used by selfish people wanting to universalize their selfishness, but beyond that is the observation that the universe, at least our part of it, is simply not set up that way. It is not interested in human self-doubt or vanity. The universe does not *expect* deed without consequence—in the case of a good deed, reward—and must regard human anxiety over such a thing as a sort of presumption. Carry my seed, eat my fruit—why would one expect one without the other? Bake the best pie, get the blue ribbon; kill the cave bear, have your name given to a warrior god; stand before the lions, take the martyr's crown; be kind, go to heaven. The inevitability of this exchange is practically Newtonian; if this, then that. Why should it gall us so when the phrase "what goes around, comes around" applies to good things, too? Of course there is altruism, for altruism is the doing of good without the conscious expectation of reward. That reward comes is not the altruist's fault, but creation's. A good deed is still a good deed even if you stand there afterward with your hand out, waiting. The flower would find your bearing

165

its seed without your sniffing its fragrance or lapping its nectar unintelligible.

I HUNG THOSE RED PLASTIC FLOWERS that you fill with sugar water on my porch to attract hummingbirds. They work. This spring they had been hanging for about twenty minutes when a female rubythroat zoomed in for a sip. Maybe she was part of last year's crowd and had been expecting them; maybe she was a migrant and, before many actual flowers appeared on the April hillsides, was using them to stoke her northward. Soon there were probably ten visitations an hour, but even that bounty did not satisfy my greed.

Looking one afternoon out the front window, I saw a hummingbird low down in the unkempt thicket of my lawn. I thought he was exploring or feeding on something when I understood that he was caught in a tangle. When you're that size the least thing can be a danger. I went out to release him, respectful of his pint-sized indignation. He kept launching himself at me as best he could, what with his tininess and being wound up in a bit of grass, his hair of beak stabbing, wings beating. When I got him free, the impression was not of smallness, but of power, zooming past my ear with real noise and a real rustle of wind, as if I had been grazed by a speeding atom.

On hot summer days I sometimes walk into the living room, to see a hummingbird hovering at the window, moving slowly across the glass, peering intently at the interior, like a diver in a bathyscaphe, cocking its eye at a foreign world. My hummingbirds evidently communicate my existence and my weakness for their kind to relatives far to the north. I must keep the hummingbird feeders up until Thanksgiving because I saw one once on that very day, beating his way through falling snow to the only source of nectar in a hundred miles.

The price tag around their spindly stems read "attracts hummingbirds," so onto my hillside went formidable stands of butterfly bush. I planted horsey, trumpety flowers, hollyhocks, foxglove, acanthus; whether they really attract hummingbirds, they look like they should. They're the sorts of plants hummingbirds are always visiting in art.

There are orchids that evolve into the shapes of the wasps they prefer to be pollinated by. I have done the same thing. A prodigy by evolutionary standards, I transformed my porch into a faux flower bed in five minutes. If the hummingbirds know the difference, they don't care. Whether I have trained the hummingbirds to respond to my artificial flowers or they have trained me to create them is presently unanswerable, but I know the exchange is as evenhanded as nature can make it.

MY CONTRIBUTION TO THE THANKSGIVING FEAST for several years was the homemade bread for which I was modestly famous. I stopped using a recipe a decade ago and simply scoop enough flour to soak up whatever liquid base I've chosen, in this case half a gallon of sweetened buttermilk. A stick of butter for shortness. Then the honey. A few cups of raw oats for texture. Yeast dissolved in honey water. Then, as it turns out, nine pounds of flour. The brute force necessary to knead that mess works out a week's frustrations.

I have used almost the whole jar of honey in the bread. The comb is left and maybe an inch or two of honey gathered at the bottom of the jar. I decide that what is left is not enough to store, and I don't have flour enough to soak it up if I put it into the bread, so I put it on the porch for whatever wild creature happens by.

At dawn, a cloud of honeybees hovers over the jar. "Good," I thought, and went about my chores. "Let it return to its origins."

When I looked again, the jar had become a tiny, golden La Brea. Bees landed on the enticing surface, could not rise again, sunk. Bees crept down the smooth sides of the jar, could not escape the downward slope and viscous pull of the honey and, as in the murderous goblet of a pitcher plant, slid in and drowned. Their fate did not dissuade their sisters, who made a buzzing cloud around the fatal jar. A few individuals managed to crawl out of the honey pool. Soaked with the golden sweetness, they couldn't fly, but staggered along the gray floorboards like cripples, or refugees in some horrible vision of war. At the edge of the porch, a neighborhood cat waited, pouncing and devouring, her prey too honeyed over to sting. The jar was black with bodies, and still they came through the air at that irresistible signal. The best I could do was shoo the cat.

Finally, in darkness, I snapped on the porch light to

see that the bottom of the jar was black with bee bodies, a community of mummies in incorruptible honey. I let the jar sit. There were six hours of darkness coming. I prayed some hungry creature would happen by and cleanse me of it. It was too horrible to think of, certainly too horrible to deal with it myself.

When morning came, the jar was gone. I considered to-ward whom to aim my thanks. I was betting on an opossum.

Refuge

IT IS AN ODD TRUTH that the more one knows about deep ecology, the less one fears the consequences of human folly. The changing shape of earth's orbit through time, the alignment of the continents and their effect on oceanic currents, the varying tilt and wobble of its axis have so much to do with the planet's temperature, and atmospheric conditions so little, that our fear of bringing on either greenhouse heat or atomic cold through our own actions is a little touching. Self-immolation is not impossible, of course, but a far more drastic calamity than seems likely at the moment. Let's keep this to ourselves, though, lest greedy people take the fact that they will not do permanent harm as license to do temporary harm, say a millennium or two's worth. Time enough, of course, to annihilate us, though the horseshoe crab would scarcely notice.

During those times when earth's orbit was especially elongated, when the axis was tilted so as to give the greatest contrast between seasons, when the continents (such as now) were arranged so as to block the circulation of warm water to the poles, the ice descended. We languish now in an interglacial period. The ices are diminished but not gone; they are almost certainly coming again. The Pleistocene saw seventeen cycles of glaciation in fewer than two million years. The previous glacial cycle came to an end two hundred and fifty million years ago, when vast stretches of Gondwana—most of Africa, Australia, India, South America—stalled over the South Pole and vanished under literal miles of ice.

North America, then drifting northward across the equator, was paradise. The last great glacial advance, the Wisconsin, tens of millions of years later, began one hundred thousand years ago and reached its greatest extent about eighteen thousand years ago, though there were local advances later—including a little ice age—that let loose in the middle of the nineteenth century after gripping the north for four hundred years. Possibly this is why Renaissance and Baroque paintings of European winters are so much direr than the European winters anybody living experiences. At the worst of it, the Wisconsin ice was two miles thick over Hudson Bay, gouging its way to a point considerably south of the Great Lakes. Sea level dropped by four hundred feet or so, and the eastern coastline of America was as sixty miles out in the Atlantic, creating a vast, wooded coastal plain over which the glacial meltwaters could flood. Alaska and the Yukon were ice free, and plunging sea levels created the land bridge between North America and Eurasia that would be so momentous in the history of large fauna on both sides. About seventeen thousand years ago, the ice began to lose its grip. Three thousand years later, the glaciers had retreated from the ocean, which was therefore no longer cooled by icebergs, which sped up the warming process considerably. Five thousand years later the ice had backed into Canada. The glaciers cannot be said really to have surrendered until about six thousand years ago—by which time the Sumerian city-states were already venerable, Cypriot and Cycladic mariners already seasoned. *Homo sapiens* has never known a moment free of the glaciers. The drying cycle that thinned the African forests and sent us upright onto the widening veldt is part of their story and the beginning of ours.

I love this stuff. I love the notion of the radical transfiguration of the familiar. Death Valley was a deep, cold lake. Western Canada was swamped by gigantic inland seas. Migrating megafauna were stalled in a bowl of ice in the Yukon valley. Eastern Washington and the Columbia River were subjected to floods of unimaginable magnitude, multiples of Amazons hurtling through breaks in ice dams, gouging canyons and leaving behind stone ripples still twenty feet high. Traveling to see my niece and nephews in Atlanta then, I would ease out of the mountain snows of the Appalachians into the Georgia tundra, howling with dust and arctic winds. Southward in Florida would stretch a bitter, rainless desert. The world ruled by all this ice was surprisingly bountiful, at least in terms of meat on the hoof. Summers were cooler, but the contrast between seasons less extreme. The gazillion square miles of uninterrupted deciduous forest, which greeted the European explorers, were an impossibility, of course, but there were minienvironments, deep forests, open forests, savannah, swamp, tundra, succeeding each other over relatively short stretches of ground, so that in, say, southern Illinois you might have mastodons crunching away in the parklike woods, and a mile away, mammoths cropping the grasses of a miniprairie, all filled in round about with squirrel and deer and elk and saiga antelope and camels and lions and beavers the size of bears, and short-faced long-legged running bears near the size of rhinos. On the horizon, always, loomed the blue-white misting palisades of the Ice.

The plants of an ice-age forest would be familiar to us, though mixed in unexpected ways. The animals would not be so familiar. They were bigger, and there were more of them. Variety and adversity go together even in purely biological contexts. Even in the darkest times, when the ice sheets were at their worst and the Mississippi ran milky gray with freezing silt, and bitter wind scoured the hills of the Antilles, there were still sanctuaries. Between the

174

glaciers and the desert, at the southeastern prow of the Appalachians where the Joyce Kilmer Forest is today, huddled one of the most interesting communities of all. There would be trees. Forests. Flowers. There would be a refuge.

AMONG THE TOP CHOICES when I acquire a time machine will be Robbinsville, North Carolina, in 40,000 BC. If you were hidden in the forest, it might look pretty much as it does today, a gloom of towering tulip poplars interspersed with dark green of hemlock and spruce, in spring the pale suspended snows of dogwood, water flowing everywhere, mist alternating with drizzle through the upturned golden leaves. Even the forest-loving mastodon would not come far into the forest, where he could barely squeeze between the trunks, and not even he could push them out of his way. Walk outward a little, and the forest thins to a tree-studded savannah. Where the protection of the mountains fails, where the everlasting gales hurl needles of ice down from the glacier, there is tundra, stretching dry and bleak down toward Florida, teeming, nevertheless, with steaming hordes of reindeer and musk ox. I would be taking my refuge in the refuge of the trees, of the flowers, of herbs growing timidly by the cold streams. When the ice began to yield, the trees began to move—migrate as it were, with what might at once be called immeasurable slowness and surprising speed—northward into opening habitats, crowding out the infinity of spruces that had ruled the edges of the ice. With them came the flowers and herbs that huddled under their limbs. With them came the spring.

Each species was sheltered somewhere as its possible habitats were squeezed and diminished by the ice—on nunataks, bare peaks high enough to stab through the glacier, and, if still pretty terrible, a little wetter and more hospitable than the deserts of ice: at the southern edge of the Appalachians, between ice and desert; at the mouth of the Mississippi, deep enough in the Gulf of Mexico to remain freeze free; on the coastal plane, at the edge of the sea, in primeval Atlantises now long drowned. When conditions relaxed a little, floral species marched north again, finding their right soil, right light, right latitude, sorting themselves into the forests we know today. Forests are surprisingly young and changeable. Even a climax forest is a balancing act, a snapshot, one movement of a colossal dance. The chestnut blight altered the eastern forests within living memory enough to have created virtually a different ecosystem. White spruce once ruled the Great Plains. It probably thought this state would last forever. Scientists know from taking pollen samples out of the muck of ancient ponds that the spread and retreat of tree species across the face of this continent over the last million years was, in geological terms, a melee. As Thomas Bonnicksen writes in *America's Ancient Forests*:

> Modern forests only exist today. They do not look like Ice Age forests nor do they look like forests of the future. Forests represent a loose collection of species that grow together for a time as they pass each other on their way

somewhere else. Each species arrives and departs independently from other species. Plants move very slowly; animals move more quickly; but they all continue to move either to escape an inhospitable environment or to take advantage of a new one. If they cannot move, they adapt. If they cannot adapt, they become extinct. Thus, forests redefine themselves as plants and animals continue their relentless shuffling.

This idea was a surprise to me, and yet not. I had grown up with the notion of forests as fixed entities that reach an ideal condition and then sort of idle there-forever, unless interfered with. But that did fly in the face of things I had observed directly about the world. Back home you could find apple groves and wavering hedges almost sunk in the gloom of forests, and you knew there had been a farm there, maybe even in your grandfather's time, and that what once was, was no more. Fire would take a farmhouse, and when you were in grade school there would be aspens and cottonwoods around the ruin, and when you were in junior high, black cherries and pine. In college in Hiram, Ohio, we walked to the banks of Silver Creek through a thicket of young maples close together, squabbling, briary, festooned with beggar ticks and poison ivy, that had once been the Udall's cow pasture. Beyond them, in the unfarmable valley of the creek, silver-trunked beeches and spreading oaks ruled over a forest that was open and parklike beneath, light even in summer, a paradise of fragile wild bloom in May. One of these had obviously been, the other was climbing toward the condition of, the other.

We could see it happen. We could live long enough for part of it to be visibly accomplished.

Pioneer species, of course, come from somewhere. Now, when every suburban yard is an intentionally selected ecosystem, it is not such a miracle, but even when the continent had been scoured bare, there were pockets, refuges, out of which the trees could peep and check for a change of fate. What mysterious beauty must have abided in the secret fastness of the bald cypress, in the refuge of the magnolia, ibis in the branches, crocodile at the roots, all waiting it out together.

Times change. Now it is the remnant of the Ice Age itself one scouts for: a clutch of liverworts under the spray of a Smoky Mountain waterfall, a seam in granite at Nelson Ledges, Ohio, where the sun never penetrates and the ancient cold never quite lets go; a stand of hart's-tongue fern beneath a New York cliff. I grew up within walking distance of a glacial ghost, Alder Pond. Here a colossal chunk of ice broke off from the main body of the glacier—a sort of landlocked iceberg—delved itself a declivity and melted into a permanent lake. The Midwest is littered with its like. There were lots of ponds back home, but Alder Pond felt different even before I knew that it was: wilder, older, a baby brother of Erie to the north, and dug by the same gleaming blue-white spade. Alder Pond fills the low center of a saucer that was once itself far larger in the past than today, though pretty likely permanent enough to freeze to the muck when the next ice comes. Ringed with cattails and reed bogs, its farther parts

were inaccessible until recently, when the Akron Parks
Department built a wooden causeway into the fastnesses of
the geese and mallards. I think in some ways that causeway
is a shame. When I was a kid, the far side seemed some
time else as well as some place else. The herons went there
but we never did. Though a map could tell us that the tall
hickories and tulips we saw gold with autumn were only
a couple of hundred yards in from Morningview Avenue,
the boys' consensus was that *there began the wilderness.* Beyond
that wall of trees opened all the places told of in the movies and the TV nature programs, bears and moose and, if
you go far enough, lions and cheetah and Masai dancing
in red paint.

As we learned a little more about what we were looking
at, our imaginations just got better. Mammoth and woolly
rhino drank from those waters. The muck at the bottom
was rumored to be a hundred feet deep and, like La Brea,
to have kept a ghastly record of what creatures blundered
in. Kids could fish there, and some of us did, but I was
always wary of what might come out on the end of my hook.

I WAS GOING TO WRITE that the word "refuge" has an
entirely different meaning now, but in fact it has exactly
the same meaning it always did; it is just that we, rather
than creeping walls of ice, have forced everybody into them.
There are no wild places on earth that are not to some
degree refuges, in that there is peril for creatures to leave
them and only marginal and conditional safety if they
remain. Africa, once a continent for the animals, is now

part zoo, part battlefield. It belongs to men, who suffer a remnant of the nonhuman. Regardless of our green rhetoric, we slaughter and push back what inconveniences us, even in their last refuges. We hand wring about leaving some fragment of tundra or rain forest, which once seemed—which seemed even in my little lifetime—to be illimitable. We level the homes of the bears and pumas and flying foxes, and then wax hysterical when we find them too close to our homes—which we have built on the ashes of theirs—and they have nowhere else to go. We pull out our rifles and poisons, as though we were still the ones in danger.

I have dreams about this, waking dreams, sleeping dreams, apocalyptic dreams, in which animals creep out of zoos into the streets of suddenly empty cities, denning in the silent lobbies, prowling the dim corridors, taking it all back. In London during the blitz, they killed the zoo animals to prevent their escaping from broken cages out onto the streets, where officials feared that they might be a danger to the populace. I find this hilarious—as though the flak and the incendiaries and the blockbusters were, by contrast, perils that could be lived with. But perhaps we would not do the same now.

In the distant reign of the great ice, a whirlwind or a flood in the refuge of the cypress could have ended the cypress forest forever. It would be a fossil, merely. What about an oil spill on the Alaska tundra, plutonium in Hudson Bay of the bears, a right-of-way through a migratory warbler's resting thicket? At least part of the beauty of refuge is the beauty of vulnerability, I suppose. Some could go in an hour. The last wild rhinos could be shot without much effort in the space of a single day. I have a recollection several years back of some kind of seaside sparrow being wiped out knowingly by the building of a resort hotel, the argument being that their population was so far below viable they were goners anyway. There is no limit on the taking of the Ozark paddlefish because, its only known breeding areas being rendered unusable by the building of a dam, it is statutorily extinct. Why put limits on the taking of an animal that doesn't exist?

At least the woolly giants lapping at Alder Pond were felled by God.

Still, the wild things do take refuge. I walk through my yard, tallying what would survive if some catastrophe wiped out all the mountain ecosystems and only my property remained. I made a mistake when I cleared the brush out of the back terrace: the towhees went away and have not come back. But I still could provide a pair of nesting catbirds (not to mention three real cats, though their being neutered casts doubts on their futures as Noahs of their race), at least one fat opossum which probably lives in my tenant's crawl space, a platoon of squirrels, a few chipmunks, an enduring nation of ants (the same ones I tried to burn out once upon a time), robins, jays, cardinals, titmice, goldfinches, hummingbirds, discreet and neighborly moles. Surely my huge sweet gum pours out enough of those starry seed burrs to repopulate the world. I have an ornamental pear, which, though exceedingly beautiful, seems to be sterile. My beautiful fir produces viable cones though, and I could fill a quota of hemlock, white pine, butterfly bush, rosemary, lemon balm, three kinds of mint. Things get a little exotic after that; if you were looking for a world chock-full of lupine and crown imperial and bleeding heart and black hollyhocks and assorted greenhouse wonders, I could provide. Still, I have a better selection than Hawaii did when it rose from the sea. I don't see why I couldn't grow a paradise, too, given time.

EACH TIME I VISIT MY SISTER'S FAMILY, I see that my niece's menagerie has grown. Rebekah has a tank holding a beautiful green snake, which not only suffers but seeks human caress. She has an aquarium that holds five different kinds of turtles, including two tiny snappers, mud turtles, sliders, painteds, a couple I have forgotten, but which she knows exactly. The fish tank in the basement runs through populations according to who is eating whom at a particular time, but the constants seem to be a swarm of streamlined blue-gold catfish, far more beautiful than they would ever be in their accustomed mud wallows at the bottom of green water. All of these creatures have come from a pond dug as an attraction to a housing development in Alpharetta, Georgia, fed and drained by a single little creek, running through nothing but miles and miles of houses, so far as I can tell, and yet the variety of life in it is bewildering, apparently inexhaustible. You walk to the pond at certain times and a great blue heron is feeding on the bounty. Migrating geese stop and befoul the grass before flapping on. My niece claims to have seen otters, and I have learned to trust her observation. There are certainly muskrats, five or six different kinds of snakes, and an alligator snapper bigger than I would want to encounter on dry land. If I had to guess what would be in such a pond I would say, a few crayfish, maybe. Some frogs. I would have been wrong by practically a whole ecosystem.

HIKING DAY IS, INEVITABLY, given all that I have said, refuge-checking day. I never thought of it that way before, before the bitter awareness of the passing of things, but now it will be hard to shake the image from my mind. I still find myself pretending this is a wild planet. I expect wild things, though luckily I am easy to please. It can be a grouse, a red squirrel, a pileated woodpecker calling from a tree island in a wooded valley, but it must be something.

People have occasionally noticed that my weak eyes, and consequently my formidable eyeglasses, do not keep me from a kind of morbid alertness in the wilderness. I'm forever lifting the fronds of ferns to show the ripening sorii, or zooming in on a brown beetle passing through the brown leaf meal, or tweaking the sporaphytes of moss to release the invisible generations. "How do you see that?" is the question. The answer is, "Because I know it's there."

If someone ever took the issue to the next level—"How do you know it's there without having seen it?"—I wouldn't know exactly what to say, short of recourse to mysticism. What I might venture, though, is that my acuity in the forest has something to do with my central occupation as a poet. It never occurs to me to wonder how a poem comes or where it comes from unless I'm asked, and, when asked, it surprises me to observe that it comes as a sort of music. Poetry announces itself to me as a rhythm to which a tune might be set, a tune to which words might be set, though the relationship to sound must be understood as metaphorical, for it all happens only in the profoundest silence.

When I consider how I know what is around me in the forest, the same answer forms. It is not a matter of the eyes. It is less a matter of the brain than of the ears, though I must hasten to add I don't mean the pink tabs on either side of my head, but rather an inmost ear, the same ear Coleridge used to hear his Aeolian harp. Perhaps if I were a fish I could reference my lateral line, but lacking that, the issue must remain a little diffuse. I can't prove I hear the difference between two birds that have neither called nor shown themselves, but I think I do, as if some plenum communicated through itself the texture of owl's down and crow's feather with absolute distinction.

Today the sky is blazing blue, each leaf on each tree on the surrounding mountains distinct, as if gems had been cut by lasers. We owe this lucidity to Hurricane Ivan, who blasted through and took with himself, along with roads and trees and roofs, the muck that had been clouding our air since midsummer. As I paced the rooms of my house in the darkness of the storm, waiting for a tree to crush me, waiting for a bolt to set me aflame or a wave out of the deep to bear me away, I looked out the front window and noticed that the hummingbird feeders were, miracu-lously, still in place. When the wind finally died, they were there still.

I thought that a signal victory, until a certain rhythm began to reach me from the air. It was a rhythm not of presence, but of absence. The tubes of sugar water that nourished them might have ridden it through, but the hummingbirds were gone. I knew this by a change in the music, an alteration in the pressure of air no longer beaten by that blur of wings. It had been three days, and no emerald body returned to the feeders. I stopped look-ing. I really hadn't needed to look at all. Where would a hummingbird go in that juggernaut of wind and rain and darkness? How could it keep its little furnace alive and not be beaten to atoms in the tumult of the air? I kept the feeders out, though, and before long some of them came down from the north and needed a little nectar—mine or the hollyhocks'—to stoke them southward. Be-sides, I might be wrong about my own two quarrelsome males and their consorts. I do not think so. I sit here, lis-tening, ready to leap up and look out the window at the slightest modulation of the tune.

Splendors

THAT NIGHT NEAR SYRACUSE, over the snow, in the diamond-sparkling cold, opposite the moon, a night rainbow, pale and dark at once, a dark fire, a scatter of gems on purple cloth.

THAT DAY IN THE MUSEUM OF MODERN ART, when I climbed the stairs, turned a corner, and saw van Gogh's *Starry Night*. One sees this painting in reproduction everywhere. The original could be a little disappointing in person actually, so small among the often huge and vivid modern paintings, easy to slip by. But when I saw *Starry Night*, I stopped dead in my tracks. Tears flew from my eyes, and had I not been able to exert some self-control in the hurrying crowd, I would have wailed. I would have fallen to my knees. My stomach felt as if it had been punched. I had to scurry to a dark corner and straighten up. The experience of the painting was one of the most painful moments of my life. I walked away, looking at other exhibits, but always returning to *Starry Night,* each time with renewed agony and renewed desire. When I went home that evening I thought about what had happened, trying to identify the emotion that nearly doubled me over with pain. At last I knew what it was. I'd felt it before in lesser degrees. It was homesickness. Not of a boy away at camp for the first time, but of Lucifer hurled out of heaven. Through the painting, not really my eyes but my emotions had sensed a world once available to me—beautiful and clear and holy—which I had wandered from, keeping from it only the sadness of regret. I was homesick. Something in the painting, in the *beauty* of the painting, reminded me of home, though of what home I am still at a loss to tell.

This sense of regret happened with a Bellini Madonna in the High Museum of Art in Atlanta. This happened stepping inside Canterbury Cathedral. This happened when I stood before Picasso's *Night Fishing at Antibes,* before Jack Yeats's *For the Road* in Dublin. I don't see any relationship among them except that they were all remembrances of home.

OR AGAIN: I attended an evening of concert arias at Severance Hall in Cleveland, featuring the local winners

of the Metropolitan Opera auditions. Just before intermission two strapping young men walked forward to sing
the male duet from Bizet's *The Pearl Fishers,* "Au fond du
temple saint." They were but briefly into the music when
I felt movement beside me. I looked over to see the man
in the next seat bent forward in a posture of grief so extreme that only the word "sublime" covers it. His lips were
drawn back in the shape of a scream. His eyes did not drip
but streamed tears. He was trying to keep quiet, but every
now and then a whispery echo of a moan was audible,
oddly harmonious with the music of the two boys. After
intermission the seat was empty. I don't know what was
happening inside him, but I'm sure it was occasioned by
the music. Like me staring at *Starry Night,* he had been reminded of his ancient home, with a pain and a longing—
and, oddly, a joy—that was past enduring.

Most art is created out of grief, even if the artist seems
to himself at the moment of creation perfectly happy.
Whatever else a work of art might be, it is a corridor between worlds: the world where the pain originates and the
world where it is healed. I do not have the vocabulary—
or the present will—to prove that the apprehension of
beauty is the sudden recollection of one's true self in
one's true home, but I base my life on the truth of it. We
are Blake's midgets, caught at the limits of contraction,
catching glimpses of ourselves as star-brushing titans.

THE SKY IS STILL GREEN GRAY, a high wind moaning in
the tips of the trees, a day and more now after the slamming

through of Ivan. I have all the lights on, and the CD playing Rococo opera, tapping away at my computer, just to revel in having power again. I will probably sleep with the light on tonight. We got fringes of hurricanes in Ohio once in a while—Donna, I remember—but I thought they were just a line of especially vivid thunderstorms. DJ and I watched Ivan on the Weather Channel Wednesday night as it poised to strike Mobile. I kept saying, "It's not coming here." Thursday afternoon I went down to All Souls Cathedral and helped lift everything off the floor to the third or fourth shelf, in case high water came. I told everyone it was a false alarm, but I kept lifting, because I wasn't sure. My nature is such that I have refused to cry wolf from time to time even when the wolf was at the door.

Thursday night, Ivan came indeed. The lights went off at about 10:30. What followed seemed to be an eternity of dark and noise, though of course it couldn't have been any longer than the hours on the clock. It was impossible sleep; I was up most of the night. When walking circles in my own floor grew old, I put on my yellow slicker and went out into the storm itself. The trees were swaying like grass. The mountains were great dark harps, roaring. My colossal sweet gum seemed rocked by a series of explosions. Green flashes were sometimes lightning, sometimes exploding transformers, plunging some new part of the city into deeper darkness. What surprised me was that the hurricane was warm, like a flying bath. I liked that part. Waves of wind-driven rain swept like surf across the parking lots. A pine split and sailed into the street, all but grazing the tips of my toes. I stood there and watched it, wondering, "Is that thing going to take me out?" until the second when the question was answered. Tremendous, roaring majesty, an exultant god whirling in the air. I stood in the middle of the Wachovia Bank parking lot, the waves of watery wind coursing around me, the hemlocks bending almost to the ground, and I felt so solid; I felt like the earth itself, immovable, maybe, in an unfathomable sort of way, merry, with the great wind roaring around as though we were complimentary powers come to visit each other at the edge of the world. It was stupendous. One doesn't get to use that word very often, "Stupendous."

I startled my neighbor Zack when he came out with a flashlight to inspect his porch, and I called his name out of the whirlwind. I hope he was afraid it was God.

I was, however, also frightened, in a way I'm not used to. Dread filled my heart, chest-clutching dread. After the dread became too deep to endure, I began to analyze it, and realized that I was not actually afraid for life or limb. I was afraid for my *stuff*, afraid not really of losing my possessions, but of how to deal with things once they were gone: which professional to call, what nail to nail, what knob to turn. I have never known how to handle problems with possessions. I dreaded the bother that would accrue when everything had to be fixed. Once I realized that, I was able to lie down on the couch and sleep a little, the bewildered cats pressed against my sides. Every now and then, in a tremendous gust, the black walnut tree above my bedroom banged the roof with profound and resonant percussion.

But, morning came, even after that night. The air was filled with the incense of shattered pines. My neighbor's basketball hoop had been uprooted and launched through a back window of my Explorer. In truth, what surprised me was that the damage wasn't worse. Wind like that, rain like that, should have obliterated the world.

I AM WALKING THE ROADS around Hiram, Ohio. Pioneer Trail slopes so that the ground meets the blue spring sky as though it were the final curve, the end of the world. Apples are blossoming in the surrounding farms: diamond and emerald sealed in a sapphire dome. I am so full of animal exultation that I don't know what response to make—except to note, for the first time, that the exultation is not just animal, but angelic as well, animal and angel in one moment, the swift beast and the blazing spirit. I lift my arms into the wind. What must the farm wives think, peering from their windows? I hear a sound in my throat, and the sound is my praying that I might have mental access to this moment forever.

NICK, MY TRAVEL COMPANION, and I round a bend in the road and come to the town of Dunquin, County Kerry, the westernmost point of the elder world. It is sunset. The sun has touched the edge of the sea and set it afire. The green sugar loaves of the Blasket Islands float on a sea of red-gold flame. I know the natural causes of the splendor, but what I see is an angel standing in the sun, his fire so bright he casts a shadow on the light behind him. Nothing is tied down. The islands, the sea, the little town, the twilight-blasted sheep, break their moorings and ascend.

SNORKELING OFF BERMUDA, I'm rising up one side of a coral boulder as a parrot fish nibbles his way up the other. We meet at the top, staring suddenly into each other's eyes. What he saw must have been disturbing, for he was gone in an instant, simply vanished into thin blue water, no mean feat for a creature three feet long and as heft as I. But what I saw was living jewel, silver and ruby and sapphire set in a jangled fabric of azure, indigo, and moving light.

IN THE CONSTELLATION OF THE SWAN, two galaxies collide, one passing through the other, making an X in the sky. So many jostling fires, so many billions of lights that the throat tires just saying the number. Out of the collision, at the axis of the intersecting shapes, come jets of energy, gold star fire fountaining millions upon millions of miles into the blackness.

MY PEAR TREE, snow-white by the April moon, a hill of white under the floating pearl of white, a bird singing in it wakened suddenly, by me, perhaps, or so deep in a dream it doesn't know it's singing.

A SOUND AT MY LIVING-ROOM WINDOW on a summer night—I rise, thinking it's a student or a friend playing; I walk out onto the porch. There's no person there. What there is, is an imperial moth, enormous, milk white, its patterns obscured by the dark, attracted by the lights of my living room and beating, however gently, against the glass. I reach out to hold it in my hand. It allows me. It spills over my hand on all sides. It has real weight, not moth-like at all, fluttering with the strength of a bird. A fine white dust begins to cover my fingers. I turn it away from the bewildering window, aim it into the night, and let it go. It beats away, owl silent, so huge I can see it a long time against the wall of stars.

I'VE CLOSED MY GALLERY—a dream of seven years, finally a failure—and am storing the last remnants in one of those rented storage sheds. The storage sheds are in a large field between the river and the rising hills that become West Asheville. It's night, a bow of moon low down in the east. The bow-new-bent-in-heaven is my favorite moon, and I try to brush aside exhaustion and discouragement in order to give it full attention. As I focus on the moon, something rises from the black scallop of trees on the horizon, between the sheds and the river. It nears and swells. I see it is white. I am in the mood to think it is a ghost, but it is instead a barn owl, heart faced, ghostly, so silent that had I not been looking in exactly the right place, it would have passed unnoticed. As it nears, it dips down out of the sky, crosses the bow of the moon, and comes straight at me. Down it comes, hurtling silent through the air, but I stand my ground. It drops so low that when it passes, I feel the wind of its wings in my hair. There was no reason for it to drop so low except to have a good look at me. I hadn't realized how big a barn owl is, the spread of its wings blotting out the bottom of the sky. Whatever was bothering me flees away. I breathe out two words into the night air. I breathe out *Lord God!*

IF YOU ARE SAD and at war with God, and happen to be in Galway, you might take a walk out along Nimmo's Quay. The rain forms a tunnel around you, and whether the tunnel is real or a trick of the city lights is impossible to tell. You walk on, and it opens in front of you, a lesser dark opening onto the greater dark of the rain-pocked bay, lengthening before, closing up behind. You catch movement out of the corner of your eye. You whirl and see a heron settling down on stones in the shelter of the quay. The heron speaks. You have been told that the herons speak in a harsh, prophetic voice, mostly at night, but you have not believed it. The heron is a gray ghost in the blackness, a silhouette when he moves against the lights of the Long Walk, and he is saying . . . something. You walk toward him. Two steps. Ten steps. You could touch him if you dared. It doesn't matter how close you come. He will have his say. The likes of you will not disturb him until his prophesy is finished. Then another dinosaurian shape flaps out of the darkness, and in a minute more, another, and another. Sixteen, maybe more at the edges of the light. The herons are coming from the face of the sea to rest on the shore by night. The herons are coming from the face of the sea to prophesy, and you alone are there to hear.

At first you despair, because you don't know what they are saying, and the fact that they are saying anything at all is so remarkable that each sound must be precious, must be, like Sibyl's leaves, a catastrophe to lose. The squawk and groan. You stand and listen in your tunnel in the rain. Then, when you think it can't be darker or sadder, what with the storm and your loneliness and the sad voices of the herons, you realize you have misinterpreted everything. The herons are singing. They have come home to rest between the sweet loud river and the solid land, and the rain can fall as it will. They have spent the day gleaning the deep, and now they are home, and they are telling the story of the time, and they are telling it to you. Whether you understand or not is immaterial. Someday you will open up your mouth, and the croak of the heron will come out, and you will hear, somewhere, the closing of a golden circle. You head back toward the town. The herons rearrange themselves a little to let you pass, but cannot be startled back into the air. The pubs are still open. The streets are still full. The rain is a set of fingers, pushing, prodding, as a sculptor shaping now hard rock, now the green wave, now the wayward, half-yielding, half-adamantine flesh of men.

I'VE COME ON AN OFF DAY to the Jackson, Mississippi, zoo and find myself alone at the rhinoceros enclosure. The rhinos are listless, red with the dirt they've been wallowing in. I look around to see if anybody's near, and nobody is. I begin to sing to the rhinos. I sing "She Moved through the

Fair" and "The Leaving of Liverpool." The rhinos move to the edge of the enclosure, right beneath me. I sing "Kevin Barry" and "The Girl with the Nut-brown Hair." The rhinos are listening, their heads still, one of them with its hoof bent in the air like some huge dancer. They are listening to me. It is the most amazing thing. I know I must keep singing until someone comes, that I must extend the moment until it cannot be extended.

LONGISH HIKE in the penetrating summery light. It was the third of January and I was hiking at four thousand feet in a T-shirt, sweating. What world is this? How do the creatures of the glaciers cope? Winged grasshoppers flew up from the path. As I sat and wrote in my journal, an inchworm measured its way across my pant leg. I'd never invested in the maps that would tell me exactly where I was on the mountains, but I started north from Ox Creek Road (Parkway "north"—the actual direction, I knew by the constant blaze of sun on my right hand, was east) down one terrible steep mountain and up another in long, lazy spirals. I ate an orange and tossed the peels behind a stump, thinking they would rot away unseen, but when I'd gotten up a few more rungs of the spiral, I looked down upon a blare of orange, visible, evidently, from every corner of the wilderness but the one where I had been standing. I leaned for a while against the lee of a great oak, incredibly, to get out of the blast of sun. The parkway ran several hundred feet below, closed to cars, disturbed only by the whirring of bicycles. The inchworm relocated to the page where I wrote, contrasting with the shimmer of white paper. Then he was on my thumb, where he progressed without my feeling him at all, not even the tingle of hairs. All was new ground for me, a new penetration, though I have done most of the trail southward and at least some of it farther north. I had lost my cherished New York City Police baseball cap coming up the trail, but going down I found it dangling from a branch over the trail where someone had hung it for its happy owner to find. How startling the human colors dark blue and orange and flat dye-green are in that wilderness of infinite modulation.

WHITE SPRING BEAUTY and pink spring beauty, the white violet. The Canadas trumpet over Alder Pond, neither settling nor soaring, ecstatic and inconsolable, in one last winter cry.

For half an evening I took the geese to task for their hysterical lament. *Settle for the night, or brave deep heaven and be done.* I walked to the brim of the cold lake and cried to them, "Enough!" Then the ones that had been crying and the ones that had been silent rose, all rose and made their orbits between the lake and sky, neither tightening nor letting loose, circling and crying, a cyclone feathering the water backward from the downstroke of their wings, and I realized they were answering me, that my voice through the forest had become the song it would fall forever short of singing: a thunder of April on the troubled water, in-consolable, ecstatic, my lion's head to theirs thrown back at sunset, roaring.

I had cried in goose, "desire." Then they came beating with black wings, ceaseless under the first four stars.

I'M WALKING TO SIAMSA at the Claddagh Hall in Galway. I stop for a rippling motion in the river. It is a seal, fishing at high tide, its huge brown mermaid eyes looking into mine with mutual curiosity. Over the seal's head a heron flies. Under the seal, the fins of shoals of fish flash and burn in the slant, green-penetrating twilight. The moon is a crescent in the indigo sky, a melted crescent on the rippling waters. A child's voice cries from the riverbank, seeing what I see—

As I stand in the blue rain hitting Galway Bay, the tide turns in sudden shimmering light. I hear such silence, see such immense darkness. Then comes another sound, low and harsh toward the lights of Salt Hill, then under the amber quay lamps flaps a gray heron—dark gold in that light. Then there is another heron, and another, all croaking in their night voice, seven in all, heading for a strip of beach uncovered by only that much fall of tide. The herons cross and recross the river, so low that one cannot see them against the lights, and know of them only by knowing.

The bars are closed when I come back into the world, so there is no one to share this with.

BESIDE THE RIVER CHERWELL in University Parks, Oxford, England. The moorhen and the moorcock and their five soot-ball chicks pad upon the water lilies, the white water lilies and the pink. The moorcock warns away the too close geese. The moorhen teaches her chicks "light" and "cool" and "water lily" in their bell-like, untranslatable tongue.

A black dog sleeps beside the water.

The black dog wakes, plunges, swims. Ripples raise the water lilies, slam them down. The moorhen and the moor-cock and the five dark chicks disappear as though they never were. The striped tigers of the deep stampede their silver quarry—the big fish and the little fish, I mean—and the face of the river dimples, flashes, then goes dark.

I think this time everybody's safe.

Everybody found some niche in time.

Then when the stream goes calm, I see the long shadows under water, slim shadows that are the hunters' bodies, broad shadows that are their interruption of the sun in its descent. They are famished, having failed. Wait-ing. Then their shadows enter mine. I move away, edible, and afraid.

What does the lone goose, sitting on the river, the lone goose with the green light under her and the blue and white above, the lone goose with her head cocked so the sun makes topaz of her visible eye, what does she think, suspended there between a light and a light? Her flock is fifty yards away, where some child is throwing bread. She let them go. She waited till the silence closed around her, for the visitation of the sun to her golden eye—between the emerald and the sapphire, head cocked, thinking what? paddling, then still—in the breath between the utterings of the river.

The land from the ordered water must seem chaos: those giants casting to and fro on their long legs, shouting, sitting, running, taking out their books, putting their books away. Unlike the moorhen and the fish and the still trees, there was no one at the morning of all things—to tell them what to do. See how some rush here and some rush away? Some sleep in the long grass, and the finger of dreams points at the spot in the river where the sun at noon rests for a moment at the soundless bottom.

The Catamount

My eyes have caught something in the hard mountain light. The mountain goes away; for the moment I see only a hue and a texture out of place, a "wrong" thing in the harmony of stone and sky. After a considerable time I realize that I'm looking at the gnawed-dry hide of a deer surrounded by scattered bones and a few strands of inedible gristle.

I have been climbing in Shining Rock for several hours, having mounted from the sparkling waters of Graveyard Fields. It's early spring. The air is dazzling. Ravens fly overhead, rolling and chuckling. Their interest in the carcass is as keen as mine, though of a different nature. They have been watching me all morning, and probably have deduced that I am more fun than I am danger, that I probably can be played with. I left white cheese for them on a high rock, upon which they dived before my back was fully turned. I move so that the full blast of the sun comes from behind my back onto the dead deer. Red, blue, faintly luminescent yellow flash out from the remnants. Fuzzy raven shadows, high up, obscure the ground for an instant. Kitelike, the birds go the way the wind carries them.

The most electrifying fact is that I passed this spot yesterday, coming from the other direction, easing down into Graveyard Fields from the heights. The deer was not there. The ground is open, and I would not have missed it. This death happened to the deer in the space of twenty hours. The list of plausible predators—foxes, dogs, ravens, raccoons—will not account for it. Men? No, it is consumed throughly, not like a man kill at all. Was the carcass dragged from somewhere else? Why and by what? There are no drag marks across the yellow grasses, or none that extend very far from the body itself. The head is chewed some but largely intact. I see no bullet holes in as much of the hide as I have stomach to probe.

The wonderful, terrible words come to mind: *cougar, mountain lion, puma, catamount.*

That there were lions in these mountains is past doubt.

That there are still is largely rejected by the scientific community; however, the possibility is cherished by certain locals, such as myself. That I would be prey as rewarding as, if slightly more troublesome than, deer does not curb my delight in the possibility. It is broad daylight—the broadest daylight imaginable. The hunter, whatever it was, has clearly already eaten. There are perhaps sixty recorded fatalities to lion attacks in all of North American history. *Maybe.* I look wildly around, speculating that it would be guarding a kill, however thoroughly picked over. I can see for twenty miles on every side from that high, bare, dazzling eminence. Not even my eyes are *that* bad. Nothing.

But I will not let that "nothing" dissuade me.

I return that night with a sleeping bag, binoculars, a small blue backpack with the usual wilderness things: matches, bug spray, flashlight, plus a liter of lemon-flavored vodka—to keep off the chill, I say. I did some scouting the morning of the discovery and figured out where I will spend the night. There's a place where the headwaters of the Pigeon River narrow, right below the carcass, in sight of it but for a shoulder of yellow grass. The bank is worn there because it is the natural fording place for hundreds of yards in one direction and more than a mile in the other, the natural fording place for hikers and wild creatures alike. Tracks in a triangle of mud, along with the sucked out exoskeleton of a crayfish, tell me that the raccoons at least are habitués. I edge into a space of flat rock at the edge of the ford where creatures can get by well enough, but not without being seen. Backed into a crevasse like that, I will be at least partially invisible. Plus, I am downwind from the openings of the ford. On the same edge of the ford as I, right beneath a tiny, mossy falls, the stream opens up into a calm pool, rippling with trout. Everything must come to drink.

I have come when it is still light, and I can read a little, but night comes on quickly, beautifully. There's not much dust or water in the stainless atmosphere, so all the sunset manages is a quick splash of flamingo before it gleams over into silver blue. The moon is full. I hadn't planned that. It rises beside Sam Knob in a gold conflagration, swiftly, getting whiter as it gets higher. It makes the hill the color of distant fire, then of linen and snow. Soon the dark is not dark at all, not black, but silvery cobalt, a line of shadow thrown behind every tree, every blade of grass, moving as the moon moves. The stars—well, there's no point. What can I add to the exultation of men in starlight? The million, million stars make still points on the face of the stream until broken by the body of a trout. Some really are red, some gold, one almost green among the blue-white diamonds.

Beauty is no insulation against cold, so I begin to sip at my vodka. The taste is just right, and it goes down in citrus heat, like the starlight, cold and hot at once. I can't imagine why I haven't come to this place again and again, night after night, it is so beautiful, the interior of sapphire, a great, cool hall twinkling with lights. Perfume floats from the spruces on the far bank. My back crushes some herb when I lean into the dirt; the tang is woody and lemony.

Now, I must confess, what I was experiencing under the rising spring moon was for the most part the point of the adventure. I did not really expect to see a catamount. The soberer parts of me didn't believe there was one to see. Still, if I turned my head, I could watch the broad flank of Sam Knob gleaming in the moonlight. An owl hunted near the middle of it, a gliding boomerang of silver, banking, then dropping silent as the stars. One fewer mouse. If I could see an owl, I could see a lion, and if I were a lion, that's where I would hole up until dark, high on a pyramid of mountain where you can see in any direction the expanse of a European country.

As I sipped the vodka, the night became deeper and more wonderful, and though I have put those descriptions in the same sentence, I think it was only partially *because* of the vodka that all grew deeper and more wonderful. The moon became more compact, its light sharper, less diffuse, its shadows cruel with the clarity of a slash between ink and silver. I pulled the sleeping bag around me, building a little sling at the edge of my stone, so the edge wouldn't drag in the water. I was getting drunker and drunker. As I said, part of me really didn't expect an encounter with a lion, but the part which did suspected also that inebriation, far from compromising the event, might enhance it, might, in fact, be necessary.

Major woods lay on the far side of the stream. You'd

have to pass my ford or splash through the water itself to get from the sheltering woods to the forage in the high meadows. Deer massed on the far bank, watching me for signs of a threat. They wanted to get across, and they weren't especially keen on the unknowable black water, so after a half hour's waffling, across they came, single file, so close to me that, with a quick, catlike lunge, I could have seized one of them. They brought the smell of the trees with them from the trees. Trout erupted at the far end of the pool, reacting to the hoofbeats of the little herd. The deer paused, hooves midair, long enough, I guess, to register "a fish" and move on. It took them maybe ten minutes to pass.

Another small herd began to mass on the forest side, and I was waiting for them to get in line and come when there was a disturbance in the meadow. I heard a stamp, a scuffling sound, and then an uneven rhythm of hoofbeats. Something had startled the herd. I raised up so I could look out onto the open. Sam Knob seemed smaller in the distance than usual, as though its silver had been all this while melting into the silver of the meadow. The shrubs were edged with pearl fire, backed with the sable of their own shadows. There were no deer. I sat frozen, hardly daring to breathe.

That I heard a scream I do not doubt, even to this hour. Lots of things scream . . . a rabbit in the talons of an owl . . . something, almost anything taken by surprise . . . but this was not a scream of fear. This was a scream of triumph, of possession. *This mountain is mine. I am this mountain.* I believed

I was hearing the hunting scream of the mountain lion. The bowels loosen. The blood drains from the limbs. The knees sag. But the heart shouts *Lord God!*

I was very drunk. All that I have mentioned can be accounted for by that condition—except the scream, which I *heard*. I ran from my hiding place out onto the high meadow. Away to the left corner of the field I could see the deer, still trotting cautiously, looking blue and soft in the moonlight. To my right, much closer than the deer, a sound, a flash, a disturbance of the grasses of a long body moving. It turned away from me and headed for the Knob, holding to the shadow of a low ridge. It entered the open and was no longer dark, but shimmering white like a lake where the moon rises from it. Its brightness made it, oddly, harder to see in the silver of the meadow. It was getting away. I began to run; I began to follow the shape. Had the price of following been certain death, I would have followed. The killer, the catamount—

And at that moment, everything was completed:

I'M AT THE FEET OF SAM KNOB and I am drunk and winded. I have run up from the river across the high meadows chasing something. I cannot run another step. I bend over in the silver grass, gasping for breath. I'm mud to the knees from sloughs I had no idea were there. Cut by brambles. Skeeter bit, sweating, exultant. The lion . . . the creature . . . I look out over the moonlit expanse; there is nothing there. I turn back where I came and see the sparkle from the falls at my ford, the red eyes of the deer, moving up again to reclaim the grasslands. Sam Knob seems enormous now that I am a little way up it. I have never been to the top. This is not the night to go. I look hard. For whatever is moving there I am sober enough now to blame on the wind.

Though I had no clear recollection of getting home, I woke in my own bed. After *that,* what reason was there to spend the night in the wild? After class at the university, I drove back to Shining Rock to retrieve my gear, which I had left in the declivity in the stream bank. It was all still there, redolent of mountain herb, including the remnant of the vodka, with which I made an offering to a creek-side witch hazel. Bees and flies had found the carcass. I could see the cloud of them hovering over it, and I didn't even climb the stream bank to have a closer look.

THERE ARE SEVERAL CODAS TO THIS STORY. One is that I told some friends about the adventure, and we took it into our heads to climb Sam Knob by night. I did not promise them a mountain lion exactly, but I counted on it being in the back of their minds. The moon was no longer full, but it was yet bright enough that it lit the whole way, up and down, reddening with the thickness of the atmosphere as it sank westward. We were so loud nothing came near us, not even the red eyes of the grazing deer.

I'd set the event up as a guys' night out, but quickly realized that I was trying to finish something that did not mean to be finished so soon. I wanted to find a lion's lair, or tracks, or a sign, or another kill, but was too frightened to climb by myself. In the end, the group ascent was nothing but good fun, except for this: driving home down the Blue Ridge Parkway, the climb accomplished, I caught in my headlights at the opening of the tunnel nearest Shining Rock on the north a wildcat. Its identity was absolutely unmistakable. It was standing stock still in the middle of the road, frozen by the glare of my truck halogens, me as sober as a judge. I watched it for three full minutes until I became nervous that one of my climbing partners, moving home down the same highway and already delayed, was going to rear-end me as I sat. I turned off the lights and let the cat fade into the mountain. Had to blow my horn to get it going.

Maybe it was staring at me, too, wondering if my smell was the smell that spooked it on the meadow a few nights earlier. As I looked at the beautiful creature, even with gratitude for the sight of it, I knew one thing for certain: it had not been what I had pursued up Sam Knob from the riverbed. The feel was wrong. It was too compact, too bristly and furry. It was a cannonball, and what I had seen was a missile, long and silvery, moving more like a river than the wildcat's goatlike lope up the cliff wall from the road.

Bobcat is plenty, though. Bobcat is fine. Bobcat screams a scream bloodcurdling enough. I am content with it. Still, I do not believe that bobcat was the presence in the night. It's not that I believe—or would claim publicly to believe—that I have chased a catamount up Sam Knob. But it would be relatively easy to convince me I had pursued a ghost, or, more precisely, a vision. The American lion, the dire wolf, the slashing scimitar cats, the terrible, loping short-faced bear are gone from these mountains forever. I miss them. A creature that prowled among them, the tawny death, the catamount, still walks the earth, for a brief time, anyway. I want it, I want the creature I pursued up Sam Knob, to have been one of *them,* a nightmare of the elder world, beautiful, unanswerable, a being, or the ghost of a being, to which the only response is a whispered *Lord God.*

I HAVE SPENT A LONG TIME PREPARING. *When I am ready, I will know. When I am ready I will throw back my head on the high place; I will scream such a scream.*

The Purple Road

THE RHYME MENTIONS THE RED SKY at morning and at night, but what of the purple sky? What of this road in midair, dark purple in the west, pale, transparent purple as it rides into the east, where the sun is about to arise in glory? The hummingbirds are up early. I can see their black shadows against the purple road in the air. One tiny bully is, even at this hour, using up his energy keeping other birds away from the sugar-water feeders. I see the black shapes of invading hummingbirds approach hopefully. The Lilliputian dive-bomber zooms out from the pear tree to meet them and turn them back. Why does he bother?

There must be some reason. There must be some anxious secret in that unimaginable, speed-devil heart. The purple road brightens, but is still purple. It is almost light.

LAST NIGHT I WAS UP VERY LATE with an unquiet heart, and saw the half-moon rising long past midnight, red over the mountain. This morning the unquiet heart had not quenched itself, so I took the usual cure. I went hiking, up and south beyond Sleepy Gap, for no particular reason, other than it's where I was when I decided to get out of the car. I must have started walking with my head down, for when I looked up through the trees there was a jolt of light and space; when I looked up through the trees, there was the same moon, white and small now, in the exact center of the sky.

Usually I avoid hiking on fine summer days, assuming the woods will be crowded with the unserious hiker, but it was not so this time. The steep climb south from the Sleepy Gap parking lot is a periodic test of my physical fitness, and I did quite well, feeling strong, younger than I should, so far from winded or spent that I had to take other routes through the woods afterward to work out my energies. The forest was calm, cool, beautiful. I was, of course, agitated, but this is so common a state of affairs I bore myself with the mention of it. I picked up a walking stick.

Before me on the upward trail I could see strands of spiders' webs blocking the way, and I held the stick before me to clear the strands before they touched my body. The strands were beautiful in the light, threads of silver, gold, sometimes oceanic blue. Once I turned around to see the broken threads flutter in the breeze, but they were not fluttering, because they were not broken. They should have struck me at chest level, and the stick stood two feet higher than my head, but there they were, unbroken. I kept track after that, and whenever there was a particularly luminous thread across the path, I would raise my stick and walk through, and when I turned around the thread would have been untouched. Were the webs ghosts or was I?

I returned to the parking lot and, unspent, turned and hiked into the valley. Near the watery bottom is some of the most beautiful parkland in the world—an emerald room with a golden ceiling. It was unchanged, as I remembered it, except for the tree against which a lover and I made love long ago. The tree was not only dead, but all but rotted away, in an environment where a dead tree can stand for forty years. It is difficult not to notice such things. It is difficult not to read the signs.

I climbed off the path and found a stone under a towering butternut tree. I sat down on it to watch and listen. There was the most extraordinary silence. Once a limb fell. The limb agitated a rose-breasted grosbeak, which sang for a while. At one point I heard strong, rhythmic sounds, which turned out to be a boy running down the trail, two little dogs running before him. He disappeared down toward the black waters of Bent Creek. There was a high drone I took for a hive of bees, which I never saw. Aside from that reigned the most extraordinary silence, so silent that the light made a sound as it collided with leaves and trunks, or so I claimed to myself in that otherwise insufferable stillness. On the ground around were false Solomon's seal and cohosh and cleaver and fern and jewelweed and violet and a few mushroom-colored mushrooms, not in clumps or patterns, but discreet, isolated, as though this were someone's specimen garden.

I climbed back up and went a couple hundred yards north, but that's where there's always a pile of dirty diapers left by passersby, and the bloom wore off the experience.

When I got home I knew I had brought the silence with me from the forest. I opened the car door and quiet flowed out like a viscous liquid. I followed the flow of the quiet. It curved around the house into the front lawn, silencing and lulling as it went. There in the patch of light between trees, my red hibiscus had finally come into bloom, a flaring sun above a little planet of grass and bugs. It must have been there when I left in the morning. I must have looked past it in the unquietness of my heart. I realized it was the one red thing I had seen all day. Even had I seen the grosbeak—and I had not—the nearest his breast would come was coral pink.

Red.

Red.

Scarlet. Red.

I couldn't stop looking at it.

The moon was almost gone now. Before it sank behind the cottage it whispered into the quiet, "This is what you have to do to earn a little red. Well, you earned it. Watch for me rising by night in flamingo fire."

WHAT YOU DEPART FROM is not the way.

I was at the studio, late, after I finished the work I planned for the day, after I should have gone home. I had the brush in my hand, and I was happy. You're not happy often enough to let it slide by unexamined, so I asked myself why I was happy. The answer was this: unconsciously I was painting an essential moment of my life, a moment when I was perfectly myself and perfectly at peace. What was the image emerging from under my brush? I took a few steps back and looked. A lofty mountain range is in the distance, colored with the sun easing down toward evening. On the golden plain beneath the mountain is a solitary walker in a white shirt with a white staff in his hand. Though I had intended no such thing, though I was consciously expressing nothing beyond the movement of my hand over the bare canvas, I know the walker is I. I know, furthermore, that though the walker's back is turned and his face is set toward the mountains, the expression on his face is inexpressible bliss. I take a deep breath. I have told myself something about me.

The way I do not depart from starts at this moment under the soles of my shoes. It goes to those mountains, golden now, which soon will be blue and silver with moonlight. What will I find in the mountains? Why am

219

I so anxious to go? I don't know. So far there is only the going, not the arriving.

I'M SITTING ON THE BANKS OF COOLE LAKE in the Seven Woods, Gort, County Galway, Ireland. Lady Gregory's ruin is a memory just over the wooded hills. I have come here every time I have come to Ireland, and every time it has all but frozen the meat off my bones. I've walked whenever I could, on a long road purple with morning, or scarlet with evening, or slate gray with the heat of day.

I'm hunkered down now, with my back against the stone, delving in like an animal to get out of the blast from the North Atlantic. A swan paddles toward me, compensating for the wind by leaning hard against it on the water. The ripples of his own passage are complicated by the ripples of the wind. There is enough sun here, and the road has been long. I start up repeatedly from micro-naps as the bird approaches on the brown face of the lake. Does he think I have food for him? Am I hidden well enough behind stone and grass that he doesn't see me at all? The wind lifts the lake so that the swan rides almost on a wave, a roll of gold green under his great body. I see suddenly that there is a black swan riding under the white swan—under normal conditions I would call it a shadow, but today it is not a shadow. It has a life of its own. It seems, in fact, the true substance of the swan, while the white figure on the water is a shadow made of light.

Enough light seeps under the clouds to set a dazzle on

the water. The little island opposite my seat echoes with the beating of waves. Here the road comes to the water's edge. Farm machines cough on their way to the next field. Bullhead lilies bob on the waves, gold folded in the plies of flashing silver. The swan is coming on hard. I am an ir-relevancy. At first he doesn't see me, and then he doesn't care that I'm there. This is the way set for him. He will not depart from it. I get up and move, so he will not quail, so he will not be tempted, even for a moment, to turn aside.

I HEAR VOICES IN THE SEVEN WOODS. I hear voices sing-ing. They are the voices of the swan, the badger, the hare, the squirrel, the moorhen, and the hazel tree. This is what they are singing:

> You passing there as quiet through the woods
>
> as you know how,
>
> are you a poet?
>
> We have been sent to ask you.
>
> If you are a poet,
>
> do not write of us.
>
> Let us ponder awhile longer
>
> on the verses already laid down.
>
> Let us try to fit ourselves
>
> to those high gray words,
>
> words struck in stone
>
> as we from bone and blood.
>
> Allow us another generation,
>
> a further covering and uncovering of these hills,

to make response.

They laid us on the tables,

took our measure,

made us stay,

who should have crept away

with the mist on the lake.

We guess you are a poet.

Do not write of us.

Write of the stony paths,

the stone cities ringed with stone,

things that belong to you.

PAINTED IN MY RENTED ROOM in Sligo last night and this morning. Painted the cathedral swimming in the light of dusk, which, of course, because of the perpetual rain, wasn't there. I haven't seen the light in Sligo until this very hour. My other painting was an abstract of a salmon leaping on Lough Gill, a silver flash in the writhing, wind-torn waters. I stand by Lough Gill now. I hadn't expected the light to come to meet me here.

Two swans appear from behind the little island and sail directly toward me. Perhaps they are curious: swan anthropologists. If they come to beg food they will be disappointed. I read in a book how paleontologists are puzzled by the long neck of the elasmosaur, preposterously elongated, supple, apparently vulnerable. Obviously the paleontologists never watched swans graze the bottom with their heads submerged. An elasmosaur could locate delectables at considerable depths.

Yesterday a dog beside the lough had a large wedge of butcher paper. Every now and then he seized and shook it, reinforcing his possession of it. When people walked by he barked and feigned attack and then retreated in triumph with his length of paper. I realized that the dog was performing theater, pretending to have made a kill, then pretending to protect it from marauders who, he must have known, had no interest in his butcher paper.

This morning found me seated upon the Miscaun Medb, the tomb of Queen Maeve, on the sweetest day that I have ever met in Ireland. Across the bay, Ben Bulben snags a dome of cloud. Clouds ring the hills on all sides, though over this place is a blue dome and blazing light. Because of the weather, maybe, there's a stream of traffic on the mound. I've smiled at ten interruptions already, and I see another pair climbing the slope toward me. I carried a rock up from the valley to place on the cairn, as the queen requires. I am the lightest of heart that I have ever been upon this hill. I have nothing to say to the Power under the hill but thanks. I'll sit and listen to the birds and the hissing of the sea wind.

Later that day, deceived by my feeling of vigor, I decided to climb down Knocknarea by her sea-facing side, across the sheep pastures into the town of Strandhill. I did it in 1980, and though I remember the climb as difficult, it certainly had not been impossible. This time I didn't make it. The wide way faded into a sheep path and the sheep path lost itself in a fairy-tale forest, all dark, moist, confusing the wanderer with a maze of possibilities. I climbed laboriously back to the summit, glad for the breeze at the top. A rough-and-ready Englishman at the top wanted to know if I had climbed up that way.

"No," said I.

"Good. The guidebook says it cannot be done," said he.

I refrained from replying, "But I did it once."

Last night I walked the Garravogue to Lough Gill. The light was low and beautiful, dazzling across the waters. A rower brought his shell to shore, then launched it again, full of laughing girls he had picked up on the shore. Boys lay face down in the grass, sharing confidences, kicking the turf behind them with their toes. A pair of swans and their six cygnets sailed amid the rushes, calmly dipping their necks and feeding. Ben Bulben was a blaze of blue and gold in the distance, a tremendous will, a Wordsworthian living presence. Over all sailed puffy fair-weather clouds, white above and gray beneath, just like the swans on the water. If I were a spirit assigned to stand on the banks of the Garravogue and bless the swans forever, I would be content.

But, one must walk back to town, even from Mount Sinai, and as I did I heard some boys, about ten years old, giggling behind me. Then, with a squeal of laughter, they ran in front of me, dropped their trousers, and hobbled as well as they could for a few feet with their bare bottoms showing in the sacred light, before tearing off toward the neighborhood up the hill. I don't think they expected me to laugh, but that's what I did. It was the perfect ending to a perfect day.

WALKED FROM SLIGO TO CARROWMORE, the road a purple shadow between the green thorn and the pale flowers of the banks. I sit now in deep cool grass on the side of a hill, which I assume was the labor of the men of old. Knocknarea gleams in pale blue light to my right, filling a whole quarter of the sky. A fresh wind sings into the grass. Small birds twitter somewhere, though I can't locate them or identify them. The walk here through the country-side, past fields of curious, friendly horses, was exactly what I needed. There are two Irelands, the cities and the land, even as in ancient Ireland there was the world of light and men and the underworld and fairies. There are two worlds, wherever I am, the world of the spirit and the world of everyday affairs, and I walk the purple road between them.

The land here is rich and beautiful past telling. I stand, and as the air grows calm around me, as that space of earth accepts me as it would a stick or a stone, the innumerable lives of the land begin to play around me, birds and animals and tiny rushing lights beneath the great light. Next visit I will spend in a hut by a river and not stir away. In my next life, I will find a hut by a river and not stir away. I will wake in sight of the purple road and never step upon it. I will be home always.

Along the Sligo road grow banks of brambles. They catch at my arms and shirt and perturb me, until I notice they are not mere brambles, but wild raspberries. They are black and plump and ready, and I eat my fill, spitting the road dust back into the dust.

This moment of still, perfect loveliness, this hour of perfection—if it were my last, would I not be content? If I should cease when this gushing blue white ceases? If I should ease back into the green at my back, and sleep with my fathers? I will change my mind as soon as the wind changes.

The invisible birds are swallows. I was trying to find them in the brush rather than in the air over my head.

Heart's home, this hillside. Yes. In the deeps of time, I was here. There is now no sharp hunger to possess: I possess no longing for home, for I am home. Belonging like a calm, blue jewel, deeper than the sea. If I could just take this with me. . . . If I could surround myself with this moment as a fish is surrounded by the water of its bowl. . . .

I am happy when I am on the road. I should recognize that by now. The one I do not depart from, whichever way I go.

I SIT IN A PARK alongside the Fergus River Walk in County Clare, clouds scuttling over, threatening rain. Last night's wardrobe is still dripping in the room from last night's rain. The giant begonias filling all the flowerpots this year drop their blossoms on the walk, great messy balls of boiled shrimp pink and scarlet and butter yellow and ice white. I walk the path until it comes to a bridge, and on the other side of the bridge the Fergus flows through the wild, trees on one side, a wild verdant meadow on the other. My heart is filled with such longing, such indescribable (and unaccountable) recognition. My left leg is in such agony that I cannot climb the gate, but I stand, staring, knowing that something belonging to me lies beyond the next bend of the river. I cling to the cities of Ireland because the cities I can leave. The country of Ireland I cannot leave without the needle in the heart. I am trapped in a time that is past, yet seemingly available, like a garden in which one met one's great love and then returns to the garden and all is as it was, down to the prints of bodies in the grass, but the love does not return.

I hobble out again at evening, come slowly to where the roads cross and head out again west and north into the empty places. I catch a vision of myself as the crows flying over must see me, a white figure at the roadside, a flame, almost, beside the purple of the road. The figure takes a step on the purple road, then another, north and west into the wilderness. The figure's head is thrown back. It is singing. Not all can see his face in that light, but those that can will know it is suffused with, it is altered past recognition by, joy.

Acknowledgments

FOR THEIR CONTRIBUTION to the accomplishment of this book I would like to thank Emilie Buchwald of Milkweed Editions and the readers of my earlier work in this vein, *A Sense of the Morning,* who encouraged the helpful and entertaining and frowned sternly upon the mendacious. I would like to thank my students for their witness that there is always something to learn and always someone to teach. I would like to thank Dennis Taylor and David Factor of Hiram, Ohio, for taking me birding long ago. I would like to remember my mother for never calling me home from the woods too soon. I would like to remember the superb artist and excellent friend, TL, who inhabits this book and who died between the writing of it and the publication. I would like to acknowledge the people of Sligo for keeping the old magic alive and the people of Galway for making the magic new. I must remember the grassy slope at the mouth of Galway harbor, where the Corrib meets the sea in a blizzard of swans, where, if I do not do my best actual writing, my spirit does its best preparation.

DAVID BRENDAN HOPES hikes frequently in the Pisgah National Forest and along the Blue Ridge Parkway. The author of *A Sense of the Morning* (Milkweed, 1999), he is a professor of literature and language, humanities, and creative writing at the University of North Carolina in Asheville. He holds a Ph.D. from Syracuse University and has written two poetry books, *The Glacier's Daughters,* which won the 1981 Juniper Prize, and *Blood Rose,* and two books of nonfiction, *A Sense of the Morning* and the 1999 memoir, *A Childhood in the Milky Way.* His work has appeared in the *New Yorker, Audubon Magazine,* and the *Sun,* among other publications.

A SENSE OF THE MORNING:
FIELD NOTES OF A BORN OBSERVER
David Brendan Hopes

ARCTIC REFUGE:
A CIRCLE OF TESTIMONY
Compiled by Hank Lentfer and Carolyn Servid

THIS INCOMPARABLE LAND:
A GUIDE TO AMERICAN NATURE
WRITING
Thomas J. Lyon

A WING IN THE DOOR:
LIFE WITH A RED-TAILED HAWK
Peri Phillips McQuay

THE PINE ISLAND PARADOX
Kathleen Dean Moore

THE BARN AT THE END OF THE
WORLD: THE APPRENTICESHIP OF
A QUAKER, BUDDHIST SHEPHERD
Mary Rose O'Reilley

ECOLOGY OF A CRACKER CHILDHOOD
Janisse Ray

WILD CARD QUILT:
THE ECOLOGY OF HOME
Janisse Ray

BACK UNDER SAIL:
RECOVERING THE SPIRIT OF
ADVENTURE
Migael Scherer

OF LANDSCAPE AND LONGING:
FINDING A HOME AT THE
WATER'S EDGE
Carolyn Servid

THE BOOK OF THE TONGASS
Edited by Carolyn Servid and Donald Snow

HOMESTEAD
Annick Smith

TESTIMONY:
WRITERS OF THE WEST SPEAK ON
BEHALF OF UTAH WILDERNESS
*Compiled by Stephen Trimble and Terry
Tempest Williams*

THE CREDO SERIES

BROWN DOG OF THE YAAK:
ESSAYS ON ART AND ACTIVISM
Rick Bass

AT THE END OF RIDGE ROAD
Joseph Bruchac

WINTER CREEK:
ONE WRITER'S NATURAL HISTORY
John Daniel

WRITING THE SACRED INTO THE REAL
Alison Hawthorne Deming

THE FROG RUN:
WORDS AND WILDNESS
IN THE VERMONT WOODS
John Elder

TAKING CARE:
THOUGHTS ON STORYTELLING
AND BELIEF
William Kittredge

MILKWEED EDITIONS

Founded in 1979, Milkweed Editions is the largest independent, nonprofit literary publisher in the United States. Milkweed publishes with the intention of making a humane impact on society, in the belief that good writing can transform the human heart and spirit. Within this mission, Milkweed publishes in five areas: fiction, nonfiction, poetry, children's literature for middle-grade readers, and the World As Home—books about our relationship with the natural world.

JOIN US

Milkweed depends on the generosity of foundations and individuals like you, in addition to the sales of its books. In an increasingly consolidated and bottom-line-driven publishing world, your support allows us to select and publish books on the basis of their literary quality and the depth of their message. Please visit our Web site (www.milkweed.org) or contact us at (800) 520-6455 to learn more about our donor program.

INTERIOR DESIGN BY CHRISTIAN FÜNFHAUSEN

TYPESET IN MRS. EAVES REGULAR 12/15

BY STANTON PUBLICATION SERVICES.

PRINTED ON ACID-FREE 50# FRASER TRADE BOOK PAPER

BY FRIESEN CORPORATION.